ROCK YOUR
WORLD WITH
THE DIVINE
MOTHER

ROCK YOUR WORLD WITH THE DIVINE MOTHER

Bringing the Sacred Power
of the Divine Mother
into Our Lives

SONDRA RAY

New World Library
Novato, California

New World Library
14 Pamaron Way
Novato, California 94949

Cover art by Francene Hart (www.francenehart.com)
Interior design by Madonna Gauding

Library of Congress Cataloging-in-Publication Data
Ray, Sondra.
Rock your world with the divine mother : bringing the sacred power of the divine mother into our lives / Sondra Ray.
    p.   cm.
ISBN 978-1-930722-75-0 (pbk. : alk. paper)
1. Goddesses. I. Title.
BL473.5.R39 2007
202'.114—dc22   2007020835

First printing, June 2007
ISBN-10: 1-930722-75-3
ISBN-13: 978-1-930722-75-0
Printed in Canada on acid-free, partially recycled paper

10 9 8 7 6 5 4 3 2 1

To you, Shastriji, I bow before your incredible glory as a fount of knowledge and bliss . . .

I praise the Divine Mother for having sent you to us.

May everything I write here be something beautiful to honor you.

My mind has been delighted in your counsel.

My rejoicing is due to your grace.

Amma

CONTENTS

FOREWORD

It is hard to imagine life today without spiritual guidance, with so many speakers, writers, practitioners, etc., all over the place. But there was a time long ago—I'm thinking three decades here—when that was not the case. At that time, those who explored the frontiers of universal spiritual consciousness were true pioneers. Their ideas were mind blowing and life altering for an entire generation, for whom such beliefs were startlingly outside the box. One of those pioneers was Sondra Ray.

I remember first hearing Sondra speak. I was living in Houston, Texas, when one night I went to see her by myself. The room was filled were perhaps forty or fifty people. In she walked, tall and beautiful with a flower behind her ear, and she simply began to speak. She spoke wisely and powerfully but with gentleness and heart. In her words and, even more powerfully, in her being, I knew that night I had found a guiding light.

I didn't meet her personally for years, at which point I tried to convey what an important impact she had had on my life. But Sondra isn't a person to live in the past, even in your past, so I've never known if she truly understood how significant that night in Houston had been for me. The path of the illumination I received from her would continue. I remember reading her book on *A Course in Miracles, Drinking the Divine.* I remember being rebirthed by her in my bedroom in California. And I have the great good fortune of receiving email missives every few months or so, even now, from some exotic place in the world, in which Sondra either asks about my love life, tells me all about hers, announces an ascension, or lets me know some amazing tidbit of enlightened information. If there is a goddess whose name means, "Awake and Hilarious at the Same Time," she has incarnated in this lifetime as Sondra Ray.

If Sondra writes a new book, I read it. I let go of my left brain and drink her in, imagining her sitting on a chair, explaining to me what to her is so obvious and the rest of us, well, maybe not so much. I have never experienced Sondra as anything other than a beam of light, either streaming at me from the page of a book or through the wondrous woman with a flower behind her ear. I have lived enough to be able to say that of all the good fortunes I have had in my life, encountering her has been one of the loveliest. Sondra Ray is a more than a woman. The word *goddess* comes to mind.

—Marianne Williamson, author of *A Return to Love*

INTRODUCTION

We all want miracles in our lives. By coming into contact with miracles, we learn *miracle consciousness*, and
then miracles can happen for us. This book is to help you
achieve miracle consciousness. Nothing real can be increased
except by sharing. The miracles in this book are real, and it is
my duty to share them so miracles can come into your life.
All people have equal rights to miracles. You are entitled to
miracles. What is needed is a state of miracle-mindedness.
This book helps prepare for that state. The miracles in this
book are not about me. I am merely the messenger for the
sacred Divine Mother, who wants you to know that she is
available to you. If healing happens from reading this book,
Glory be to the Divine Mother!

    The original spark of creation is a feminine aspect, so
we are talking about the very primal force itself . . . the
Source . . . she could be merely called the feminine aspect
of God, but some call her the supreme deity, the source of
all knowledge, that which is beyond everything. Some say
she is actually the intelligence behind matter! That is why in

India they say that there is nothing higher than worship of the Divine Mother. After reading this book, you will understand that this applies to all lands and all people.

The great saint Sri Aurobindo said that surrender to the Divine Mother is the final stage of perfection. It took me a long time to figure out that the "secret" of the saints and masters I met was just that: surrender to a worship of the Divine Mother. From this they gained real power and supernatural abilities. She is just as available to all.

It is said that the Divine Mother releases us from delusion. This is of maximum importance on the spiritual path. To make rapid spiritual progress, one must reach for the deep, called the *Ma* (the internal), rather than the *Maya* (the external). The sooner we do that, the better for ourselves and the whole planet. The more you surrender to the Divine Mother, the faster is your progress.

She will bring us to the nurturing, tender aspects of ourselves, which are so needed to solve the problems of the world today. The Divine Mother will give us the solutions both to our personal problems and to our planetary problems. We need to let her teach us now.

We want to avert catastrophe in our relationships, our bodies, our societies, and our countries. How do we deal with the shadows in ourselves and in our societies? Logic cannot always find the answer, but the feminine side of ourselves is more capable of harmonizing the light and the shadow. Extraordinary changes do take place when the Goddess is accepted. That goes for women and men alike. I have interviewed many whose lives were completely changed by surrendering to the Divine Mother. Some of those interviews are in this book.

Since the Goddess has not been an integral party of Western life for the last two thousand years, we as her children are rather maladjusted. The Goddess, or Divine Mother, would lead us in the way of natural law, wisdom, and unconditional love; however, we don't pay enough attention to this aspect of God. That may be because of old beliefs that the Goddess is pagan and heathen. This is most unfortunate, be-cause we then overlook her beneficial, life-enhancing, and regenerative powers and her offer of renewal.

Although pure formless deity has no gender, the expressions of God as divine masculine and divine feminine are like left and right hands of God. To emphasize the mas-culine more, as we have done with patriarchy, puts us way out of balance. Too often we use our bodies to rebel against the "negative mother," whereas if we could surrender to the Divine Mother, our bodies could be used as instruments to channel the natural infinite love and intelligence needed, not only to experience bliss, but to have the purest wisdom. The Divine Mother is a spiritual channel we should enjoy: who wouldn't want sexuality radiating through the whole body as a healing force igniting the being with light?

But how do we experience the Divine Mother? That is what this book is about! It is really so exciting! We must begin by expressing more appreciation to the source of life and paying homage to the highest of the high. We must let the intelligence of the entire universe be our teacher! Remember, everything we possess is a gift of the Divine Mother.

Praise to you Great Mother. Make our lives a miracle. Show us what to do and how to do it. Let us be innocent and receptive, like a child. Make our hearts your temple. I pray that this book gives people some idea of your wondrous power and grace.

Love, Sondra Ray!

PART ONE

POWERS OF THE
DIVINE MOTHER

CREATING MIRACLES

Mother Teresa said that the only thing that should sadden us is if we do not become saints. If you meditate on that statement for a long time, it might change your whole life! She was telling us that to become like saints is our duty. I had been telling people in my classes something like that, because after all the Bible says, "Be ye perfect even as God is perfect." (That is an order!) Mother Teresa wanted us all to become like Jesus: that was the light she wanted to live and the love she wanted to reflect and express, and she did that. I was very fortunate to be in India at the time of her passing. I felt so blessed to be with the Indian people during that time, as that moment was so deep. What the Indian people care about is, How can I love God more? That is why I like India so much, and that is why I have taken people there for the last three decades.

If you watched Mother Teresa's funeral on TV, you might remember that her body was laid out on a plank and totally visible from all sides, since she was not in a casket. The cameras were on her body twenty-four hours a day. They made you just look at her and look at her and look at her. We need to look at the Mother now. We need to look at the Divine Mother. Focusing on the Divine Mother now will soften our hearts. It will make us more affectionate to the children of the world, and it will make us have more kindness, tenderness, cooperation, and encouragement in our relationships and lives. It will help us to be filled with universal love. Developing the motherly aspect of God will help us feel love for all people in the world.

The sadness of Princess Diana's death and Mother Teresa's death opened hearts worldwide, and a new vibration entered into us as a result. It was kind of an initiation. A colleague of mine said it was like an *egoist shattering*. A shattering is an initiation because it opens us up. It makes us totally vulnerable. We have no defenses at that moment, and we allow the energies to penetrate us easily and deeply. Initiation is the planting of a seed. In time, as the seed germinates, we find ourselves really changed. These two women made us focus on the power of humanitarian ideals.

The Divine Mother wants to use *you* for a mighty purpose! Are you willing to be used for that? If not, why not?

To be able to write this book, I had to be shattered. I ended up in the desert to undergo the required initiation. When I put the key in the door of my friend Nichole's townhouse in Palm Desert, there was a miracle. The scent of a big bouquet of roses filled the entrance. I noticed it and did not say anything, but then my friend Janice, a rebirther who was with me, mentioned it. We both then went inside and lit a candle for an altar. We lit a candle to acknowledge her presence and express our gratitude as well as to remove darkness in ourselves. Later I chanted the "Hymn of Worship to the Mother" in Sanskrit.

That day I really came to understand that my guru Babaji had made himself the avenue for me to the Divine Mother. Babaji is an immortal *maha avatar* and yogi master (*avatar* means "descent of the Divine into matter"—not born of a woman). He is an emanation of Divine Light who, out of compassion, manifested in human form on earth to urge humanity to progress on the path of truth, simplicity, love, and service to mankind. He is the power of the Eternal Father, Mother, and Divine Child. He can assume any form he wishes and can change that form at any time. He materialized a youthful body in 1970 in a cave near the village of Hairakhan. He took conscious departure on February 14, 1984. Now he comes and goes!

First he set out to eliminate my ego; then he threw me into the lap of the Divine Mother. Some people say that you should not have a guru, because it is a go-between and there should not be anything between you and God. I never saw it that way. Since Babaji materialized a body (like Melchizadek in the Bible), he was directly from the Source and he is God. That's called a maha avatar. And that is why it took me two years to recover just from the sight of him. It blew my circuits.

Why was it, I had wondered, that Babaji's last words were "I am leaving everything in the hands of the Divine Mother"? I did not even know what the words "Divine Mother" meant. In the church I grew up in, we did not even honor the Virgin. It was very patriarchal. Babaji's words haunted me and haunted me. I had to find out what he meant.

I made a big plan for the first anniversary of his *samadhi* (conscious departure) in 1984. I decided I would visit the most ancient temple of the Divine Mother in India the following year. This was not easy, because I had to go to the very southern tip of India. The plane landed at night. I got up before dawn to make it to the temple in time so that I could see the early morning *puja* worship (ceremonial workshop service to the Divine Mother). We are talking 4 AM, so it was still dark.

I was astonished to find that the temple was underground. I believe that this temple is called Kanyakumari Mandir. I was told the temple was more than five thousand years old. When you think of the time of Christ, that seems so long ago, and this was three thousand years before *that*! Now when you think about the following incredible ceremony I am going to describe, keep in mind that what I saw there has been done every single day for five thousand years without fail. Then you will get the idea of the power of some of these very active Indian temples. This was not part of some ruins. It was the real thing, and it is still going on right now.

I remember walking underground for quite some time. I finally got to the spot where the *murti* of the Divine Mother was. Just what is a murti? you may wonder. The murti contains the living presence of the deity. You have heard of the statues of the Virgin Mary weeping perhaps. Well, that is because they contain the living presence of Mary. It is not like worshipping idols; it is the opposite. This is because the only real idol, according to *A Course in Miracles*, is the ego, and when you are before the living presence of the Divine Mother murti, your ego is slain. On occasion these murtis have been seen breathing.

Well, I tell you, when the priests pulled the curtains back and I saw how lovely she was, it took my breath away. She had on the most beautiful *sari*, and she looked real! The priests carefully took off her clothes and folded them ever so neatly. What I saw after that blew me away.

The priests began scrubbing her whole body, inch by inch, with toothbrushes and some kind of sand cleanser. Then they washed her down. For the second washing, they scrubbed her all over again, inch by inch, with some kind of sandalwood paste. Then they washed her down again. For the third washing, they scrubbed her down again, inch by inch, with some kind of powder. Then they rinsed her off again. She was glistening, all right!

Finally, they took fresh milk and crushed rose petals in it. Then they poured this rose milk over her head. When it ran down her breasts, they quickly collected it in silver urns. Then they turned to us and gave it to us to drink, as in Communion.

There were only about three other Indian people watching this with me. We all began sobbing. We were instantly rebirthed by the Mother. I don't remember much beyond that because my mind went blank. I remember the bliss, and that afterward I was staring at the sea. I just could not believe what I had seen!

I had also been told by a yogi (whom I deeply trusted) that there was a female saint in that town at times who was four hundred years old. I had no problem integrating that, because I had been studying the immortals. And in India, miracles are quite normal. However, I have absolutely no recollection as to how I found her, nor can I remember who I was with or how I left the temple. (It is similar to the man who saw twelve yogis levitating in India and then took twelve years to remember the experience.) Maybe someday I will remember the whole story.

I know I went down an alley, and there she was. She had been in silence for years, apparently. To my amazement, she was in a rather transparent form—although sometimes she looked solid, and at other times she looked like tissue paper. But the biggest shock of all was that twelve dogs were sitting around her, and all were in a circle facing her. They all looked alike to me; I thought I was losing my mind at that point, because I started thinking that they were all yogis disguised as dogs. Some people do say that when you think of the Divine Mother, you lose your mind—and that is exactly what happened to me that day.

I could not imagine what to do in the presence of such a great saint. Fortunately, I had some sacred ash in my pocket that the Indian guru, Sai Baba, had materialized for me. So I took out the paper from my pocket and handed it to her. She immediately took it and put it on the third eye of each dog! I came after the dogs. I remember her putting it on my third eye, and I cannot remember anything after that.

I did not speak of this for years because I thought people would think I was imagining it. But years later, I read a book on the female saints of India, and lo and behold, she was there! It talked about this saint who traveled from place to place with twelve dogs. One thing I always knew was that she was, in fact, four hundred years old. I also knew that she would never have let me near her had I doubted that fact. Because I did not doubt her, I was allowed to be with her.

But how was it that she became like that? Was she born that way? If she was, how did she come to be born like that?

Good karma from past lives? If she *became* a saint, how did she do it? She was not speaking, so I could not ask her. Well, Babaji used to say to us, "There is no saint without a past, and no sinner without a future." So then, anything is possible.

A Mysterious Painting

I had needed to see a female saint. This experience shook me to my roots. Most of my spiritual teachers, up to that point, had been males. Now this was going to change and I knew it. The Divine Mother changes everything she touches, and everything she touches changes. As I write this now, I am thrilled to have two female Indian saints, Amma and Karunamayi, with whom I can spend time each year.

After this profound experience, I decided I needed to go a lot deeper into this. I decided also to commission a painting of the Divine Mother for my loft apartment in Seattle. The ceilings were very high, so I needed to have a big painting. I asked Babaji's temple painter to paint this for me. She was in a cabin on a lake outside Seattle working on this painting for months.

I became afraid to look at the painting for some reason. I lost my mind. I was thinking things like, What if it does not go with my décor? and, What if I just don't like it after all this time? Then I became sure that it was going to be too much. I knew it was going to dominate everything, and I started worrying that I would not be able to think in my own apartment. I got more paranoid. I finally sent an art critic out to look at it. He stayed in the cabin a long time. All he said when he came out was: "Sondra, it is *very* hypnotic." I became afraid that I could not surrender to this painting, so I decided to donate it to the ashram in Colorado. I told my decorator to pick it up, so he did. I left on tour. But while I was on tour, he had a dream and got the message to hang it in my flat anyway, no matter what. Since he had my key, he went in and hung it.

The night when I came home from my tour, it was midnight. I opened my door and turned on the lights, and there it was! I started to cry because it was so beautiful, and then I said out loud to the painting, "Okay, I surrender."

Right then and there a miracle happened. The scent of roses filled the air for ten minutes! There were no flowers in my flat, and I had been gone for over a month. No one had stayed there. Now I was alone with the beautiful painting, and here was the Divine Mother herself giving me a *darshan,* a glimpse of the divine, like that!

Needless to say, I had some shame for my resistance, so I decided to have a special puja (worship service) done to the painting. A yogi I had met in India happened to be in town. How rare! I asked him to do a special ceremony to honor this painting, and he happily obliged. I had a few friends over, and we all lay down and rebirthed ourselves after the ceremony. Well, I was right: the painting dominated everything. But I grew to like her so much that I would lie down on the couch and meditate on her while listening to chants. Sometimes she would show me the future.

Later, the painter told me that while she was doing the painting, Babaji appeared to her, exposing his heart, and the form of the Mother she painted was sitting inside his heart! This was the beginning of very mysterious and marvelous experiences with paintings of the Divine Mother.

THE CAVE OF AURAS

I was conducting God Trainings during this period, and they convened at different power spots around the globe. One of the strongest ones we held was in Machu Picchu, Peru. The electrical power went out in Lima for three whole days just when we arrived. That was a bit scary for the group, so we rushed to Cuzco. I was excited because I had missed that part of Peru when I was in the Peace Corps. So now I was finally going, and I was wild with joy.

The night before we went up to the ruins, I had the group at a hot springs and gave them all a wet Rebirthing to prepare themselves. It was quite something in that altitude. Later in the class, when my co-trainer and I were speaking, a student who was a minister stood up and said she was seeing an amethyst in her third eye and had the worst headache imaginable. I told her to lie down in the back with a re-birther assistant and to do nasal breathing and breathe up into her brain. So she did.

Then I resumed speaking, but not for long. A block of energy moved toward me that I could not integrate at all. It almost knocked me over! I had to go lie down with the student in the back while my co-trainer carried on speaking about the crystal earth papers. The minister was having visions. She had never seen Babaji before, but she told me a man was appearing to her wearing a poncho and that she was sure it was Babaji. I said, "How appropriate, since we are in Peru!" He told her to take me to a certain place in the ruins and do a ceremony. I said, "Great, tomorrow I will follow you." I told the group I was going to try to get us in after the tourists so we could have silence. I wanted silence so she could hear the guidance and so students could have the maximum experience of sacredness. This worked! (Too bad all visitors don't stay in silence. It is so wonderful to visit temples in stillness.)

I followed the minister for quite awhile. She whispered to me, "I don't understand, these ruins have no roofs. What I saw had a roof. Could it be a cave?" I whispered back, "Yes! That would be Babaji's style." After all, I thought to myself, he materialized in a cave and I have done spelunking a lot in my life. So I whispered to the guide, "Are there any caves near here?" He whispered back, "Oh yes, you have come right near the best one." He pointed it out. He called it the Cave of Auras.

We did the ceremony with candles, and I then told the group that it was my instruction that I had to spend the whole next day there. The group wanted to hike up the mountain, so the next day, they hiked with my co-trainer. I went in the cave with Don McFarland, the founder of Body Harmony. I felt that if I went into a spontaneous process, he would be there for me. Most of the day, however, he was rocking back and forth. I was told many things in the cave, and they came so gracefully.

The things I was told in the cave have not happened yet—except one: I was told, "Go to Medjugorje, and go alone." I knew that the Virgin Mary was materializing to the children in Yugoslavia. But, due to scheduled commitments, I could not imagine how I would ever be able to go there. I was booked more than a year ahead. But I said yes, of course, and I scheduled a trip right after the Harmonic Convergence, when I was to speak at Glastonbury, England.

We were all awaiting the great day of Harmonic Convergence. Fred Lehrman, Robert Coon, and I spoke in the town hall on the subject of physical immortality to quite a large crowd—people right off the streets. That was different. Usually we only taught that subject as an advanced class where people had preparation, but not on that day. The most amazing thing transpired: People would stand up to ask questions; and their minds would just unravel before our eyes, and they would get the answer themselves and sit down. It was a marvel to watch, and it happened in every instance! We did not have to answer one question. Afterward, we got a standing ovation for fifteen minutes. What a magical day!

In India they say that only the Divine Mother grants the boon of physical immortality. I did not really understand that point when I first heard it, but I do now. After you finish this book, I think you will also understand it.

THE VIRGIN AT MEDJUGORJE

Right after Glastonbury, I was going again to the Mother, answering the direct call. The day after the Harmonic Convergence, I flew alone to Yugoslavia. I had no time whatsoever to read up on the culture or learn any of the language. When I got to Dubrovnik, I grabbed a taxi and blurted out, "Medjugorje!" One hundred fifty dollars later, I was in a cornfield, and that was all I saw: corn—just like where I grew up. I was surprised there was no town. The only thing the taxi driver could manage to say in English was, "No hotels!" "*What?*" I squealed, looking at all my luggage. He shrugged his shoulders. I just sat there. He just sat there. Then I said to the Divine Mother, "Okay, I did my part. I got here." Then the miracles started to happen again.

A little boy got into the car. He was about four years old. He said something in Croatian to the driver, and the driver took off up the country roads. I had no idea where I was going. He stopped at a farm, and the boy jumped out. There at the end of the driveway stood the grandfather, the grandmother, the father, the mother, and three other siblings. I could not figure out why they were all at the end of the driveway, as if they were expecting me. Had the Virgin Mary arranged it? They showed me to a bed, and there was no way I could argue, as they spoke not one word of English. I had wanted to fast for ten days, so I drew a picture of food and crossed it out and circled liquids. Then they all sat down and looked at me.

Everyday I would walk three miles down to the church. I noticed there were a lot of priests in the booths for confession that spoke many different languages. Well, I decided maybe I should become a Catholic for one week.

On my birthday, I was at the church. Suddenly people were pushing me, as there were so many crowds of Catholics coming in on buses. I was pushed into a small room where I was given Communion. Now, I knew I was not supposed to take Communion because I was not Catholic, but I did anyway. It happened. That night at five o'clock, I went to the apparition area, which was a kind of a library outside the church. Everyone began looking at the sun. I was told that some people see the sun spinning when the Virgin comes inside the apparition room. I was astonished to see the sun spinning myself, and I suddenly fell to my knees. Not everyone saw it—very few, really—which is hard to explain.

The next day, I decided to go to confession for the first time in my life—Catholic confession. I was nervous but I was trying to blend in. I told the priest that I had taken Communion the day before and I was not Catholic. He yelled, "You cannot do that!" I said, "Why not?" I think he was upset with me because I was a bit provocative.

That day I went and sat under the window where the Virgin appears upstairs and did my devotions. A priest came out the second floor onto the porch and I shouted up to him, "Father I am a writer and . . . " He said, "You come at five." Later I asked people what that meant. They said that I must not expect to go into the apparition room as only the Virgin decides who gets in, and besides, if I tried, I would get trampled. I went before five and got a place next to the wall so I could be as close to the building as possible. I sat under the window because that was where the priest had seen me before, but I certainly was not counting on getting in. Crowds of people pushed up against me in no time. I could not budge either way. They kept saying, "Hail Mary, Mother of God, protect us in the hour of death." Over and over and over and over. I started talking to Mary, and I said,

"Sorry, Mary, but I just cannot say that mantra. I want you to protect me in my immortality." I related to her as an ascended master (one who can materialize and dematerialize at will), which she is, after all.

The twenty-five male Catholic priests started up the steps, and they seemed to be from all different parts of the world. Well, I thought, that is appropriate. Then the same priest I had spoken to came out on the porch and called me. Wow! I tried to get around the crowd and over to the steps but there was no way. I pleaded and pleaded but nothing worked. There was only one possibility. I would have to leap straight up and have him pull me through the railing. Since I had been a basketball star in high school and since I was thin enough, I decided to try it. People thought I was cheating. It created a real ruckus in the crowd, but believe it or not, it worked. I made it. The priest pulled me through the railing at the top of the stairs, and I was escorted in and the door closed.

The Catholic priests were sweating. It was a very, very hot August day, and the energy was unbelievably intense. Suddenly one priest fainted and they pulled him out and shoved me down in his place right next to the children! I had no time to be in awe of that miracle, because suddenly a priest shouted, "She's coming! No cameras!" I watched the children closely. Their eyes all went up in rapture at the same second, and they were in trance and seeing her. The rest of us could not see her, because we were obviously not vibrating at a high enough level like the children she had been appearing to for years. But I will tell you this: we all started sobbing. And it was exactly the same energy I had felt in the underground temple in India. We were all instantly rebirthed—all twenty-five male Catholic priests and myself.

Then a sharp bolt of energy went into my uterus and I nearly fainted. I knew it came from the Virgin, and all I can say is that I lost my mind again. I don't remember much after that, except that I was being pushed out into the sunlight and when I came down from the porch, people began to grab me. They wanted me to heal them, epileptics and all. It was very intense. I gave as much energy as I could, but this went on for three days, because people remembered I had been in there. On the fourth day, I had to go into seclusion. For a whole year, I could not talk about the experience because I would start shaking too much. Finally I wrote it all up in a book called *Inner Communion*. After that I could share it, and when I did, people would cry.

DIVINE MOTHER ENERGY

I noted that the energy in the church matched that of the underground temple in India. Of course the energies would be the same, as the Virgin is another aspect of the greater Divine Mother. The Divine Mother takes many forms. In Asia, she is seen as Quan Yin and is universally loved as the goddess of compassion. In Hawaii, many have seen Pele, the goddess of fire, manifest in the form of a woman near the volcanoes. In India she is Kali, Lakshmi, Tara, and so on.

Presently, there is a reawakening of the sacred feminine in the hearts and minds of people throughout the world. As I was originally writing this section, there happened to be a page from *Vogue* magazine that was labeled "Divine Inspiration." It showed a dress designed by Dolce & Gabbana with the most beautiful imprint of the Virgin on the front. Simply gorgeous. (I wish I could have afforded it.) The Virgin was showing up everywhere—even on the glass wall of an office building in Clearwater, Florida. I went there to see it myself. Scientists had flown in from all over the world to test the glass. They tried and tried to explain it, but they couldn't.

From that time on, my relationship with the Divine Mother really speeded up! I still had no idea why this was happening to me. If I had known what was to come, I would never have been able to handle it.

ANOTHER PAINTING

One night I was preparing to hold a chanting evening in the home of my friend Nichole. A woman I did not know called me out of the blue and told me she had this painting. Her name was Velvelee, and she had been instructed to move to Alaska, even though it was winter. While she lived there in a little room with a wood-burning stove, she began receiving instructions to do a painting of the Virgin. She was not allowed to look at any other paintings of the Virgin and had to paint this according to the instructions she heard. It came out as a painting of the Virgin holding roses. When she finished it, she was told to touch the painting, and she felt the heart of the Virgin beating! She was then told to take it around the world and let others touch it. Did I want to see the painting and feel it? she asked. Well, of course I did! I asked her to bring it that very night for the students who came to chant.

When Velvelee came over, we were already chanting. She brought the painting into the house covered and took it into the bedroom and waited while we chanted. Then she told another rebirther named Rhonda and me that we should be the "catchers." That meant we should catch the people after they touched the painting, because they would be falling back. They would be falling into our arms, she said. This we did for hours on end, because there were around fifty people. So this incredible process went on and on into the night. After we caught the people, we would help them get up and go outside where they would meditate on the moon by the pool.

By the time my turn came, I was pretty activated, to say the least. I don't even remember who caught me. All I know is this was real; I felt it myself, as did everyone. Then, before I knew it, I was on the floor in a spontaneous rebirth-ing session. I cannot remember anything after that. Rhonda claims she saw me levitating off the floor, but I have no memory of such.

Since that evening, I have lost track of Velvelee. If any of you know of her whereabouts, please send me an email on my website, www.sondraray.com.

BEYOND THE FEMINIST MOVEMENT

Around this time, I was guided to spend a lot of time in Santa Fe. I was staying with my friend Emily Goldman, a Babaji devotee. She told me to go meet a spiritual guide named Beth. I walked in Beth's apartment, and before I even sat down, she blurted out the following: "Oh, *they* want you to create something beyond the feminist movement." I said, "Could I please have more information?" She replied, "No, there isn't any. . . . It has never been done." Then she told me I was entering my true destiny and that I should do a ceremony if I agreed to accept this mission. I don't remember anything else she said that day.

I set up an altar on the hearth of Emily's fireplace. I wrote a prayer to the spiritual hierarchy and my masters and guides. I wrote something like, "Well, if I was born to do this, then I accept now, but could I please have more information?" A sudden severe wind like a cyclone rushed through the windows and blew the door open, which was rather scary. I ran to the neighbors, but they had had no such experience. I took it as a huge sign that this was something very powerful, but still way over my head. After this I had a severe spasm in my left hip for two months. Fear . . . terror. What had I agreed to? I got no clues.

Finally it was the time of the year for my annual trip to India, where I take groups to Babaji's cave and ashram.

When we got to Herakhan, I told the female assistants that I needed them to support me in a ceremony. My plan was that we would go in the Ganges River to bathe each other. Then we would rub oils on each other, put flowers on each other, and pray together. Afterward we would all go into the Divine Mother's *dhuni* (sacred fire temple) and meditate. I was hoping all this would give me some answers. Well, it absolutely worked!

After the very sweet ceremony in the river, I was walking toward the dhuni, and I got the first inkling. I heard the words *Divine Mother Movement*, and it suddenly dawned on me why this would be beyond the feminist movement. For one thing, it would include men! Why of course, I thought, all the great immortal yogis I had read about (mostly men) prayed to the Divine Mother. My teachers prayed to the Divine Mother. That was their secret! I couldn't believe I had not figured this out before.

This sacred fire pit in the temple was built by Babaji himself, with his own hands. It is the second-best place to meditate I have ever found on earth (first being the cave where he materialized his body). I did an *activation* (an acceptance prayer) where I committed to the work of making *it* alive in the world, for the mission of the Divine Mother. I also prayed in the cave that I would come to know exactly what *it* meant. Then I had to go to work because I had a large group with me, as usual, and I had to look after them.

A week later, when we got to the upper ashram in the Himalayas for the Divine Mother Festival, I immediately had the opportunity to do the second activation. On the first day of the big *Havan* (a huge fire ceremony to the Divine Mother), a place had been saved for me around the fire. Usually the men go on the first day, so I was amazed my name was called. I said, "Okay, God, I do this to represent all the women in the world." This ceremony is so powerful that it changes the elements. No mistakes can be made, and the mantras are very ancient. The ceremony lasted approximately an hour and a half. Every time I made the offering to the fire and said *"Swaha"* (which means, "I offer myself"), I added, "Divine Mother Movement . . . I offer it to you, Divine Mother." I did not even know what I was saying really, since I did not even know what *it* was really going to be! But in such a case, all you can do is pray.

The third activation was at the end of the festival, when we go to Dranagiri, the ancient temple of the Divine Mother in the Himalayas. It is the frosting on the cake, so to speak, after the festival. Everyone piles in the buses, and we go on very curvy roads for several hours. Usually people have profound experiences on the trip itself. People in my group usually release a lot of birth memories and past lives on the curvy mountain roads, and they are always extremely grateful for all the breathwork we do on the roofs of the ashram.

When we get out of the bus, we must take a long hike uphill. This is considered a pilgrimage, somewhat like the hill you climb in Medjugorje where there are the stages of the cross. We were always told that great yogis and saints walked hundreds of miles by foot to get to the temple, and they would sit and meditate there for years and years. It always blows my mind to hear that. It is a very tiny temple, but there are thousands of bells hanging outside that people have placed there. Inside, I was very fortunate to be able to sit with my gurus Muniraj and Shastriji, doing puja with them to the Divine Mother direct. I kept on saying, "Swaha, Divine Mother Movement, I offer it to you Mother . . . " praying and praying and praying.

FALLING APART

In the book *Earth: Pleiadian Keys to the Living Library*, by Barbara Marciniak (who is on the cutting edge as a channel), she says that the Goddess is going to be birthed through us no matter what, male or female. She explains how important this is for the planet. "When you explore the goddess," she wrote, "you begin to value life. When you value life, you do not kill." The main thing in her book that struck me was that she stated that the Divine Mother should be the foundation for new communities and new civilizations. When I read that, I really felt happy that I was on the right track. At the same time, my own business structure began to fall apart—it was inevitable because the patriarchal aspects had to go.

There is in India the image of Tara. She had around her neck freshly severed human heads. I never could fathom how to understand that, so I read up on it. These heads represent the nooses in a person. You can hang yourself on those nooses: lust, anger, greed, envy, delusion, fear, etc. The Divine Mother chops off your head to cure you. But we are so attached to these nooses that we shrink from the Divine Mother in fear. It is important to understand, however, that she only wants to kill the false you, the limited you, the old personality you accrued in so many births. She wants the *real* you, which is quite different.

There is another image of the Divine Mother with many arms. That represents her taking your karmas. Most people wear their karmas like clothes. She wants to take them off. She cremates billions of karmas. It is said that there is no escape except by her grace.

Once in Puerto Rico, I woke up screaming because I had a dream I was carrying my head in a bag! But I later understood this dream as a very good sign. I did not want to die and reincarnate a thousand more times. I was hoping and praying I could surrender, so I said to the Divine Mother,

"Do what you want with me!" Little did I know, you have to prepare for things to fall apart. Years earlier, I had said to Leonard Orr that I was afraid that my business was falling apart. He said, "Good. The ego has to fall apart." Things would fall apart in my business fairly often, and I stopped thinking that that was bad. Something new always arose like a phoenix. I made a lot of mistakes, but at the same time, miracles kept happening.

I was in Switzerland, where I had been asked to teach a course on physical immortality. That was rare because these were all new students to me and I usually do not teach that course to students I do not know. Well, I decided, hopefully, the right people in Zurich will come. Then I received a fax from my astrologer stating that on that very day, there was a configuration of planets in a lineup that only happens about every sixty thousand years. I believe it was Sirius A, Sirius B, Pluto, and the Earth lining up. The main message of the fax was that this was a sign that the Divine Mother energy was moving in and the patriarchy would seriously start breaking up. (That was already happening in my own organization. . . . Sometimes pioneers have to go through things first to learn how to help the others.)

In Zurich, I told the group I would have to do a ceremony to acknowledge the Divine Mother using incense, flowers, and grains as an offering to the altar at the exact hour mentioned in the fax. This came right in the middle of the seminar. I told them that it was highly unusual that I would do such a thing with a new group but they could stay and watch if they wanted. Nobody left the room. Nobody could move. Nor could they move for a long time after. It was stunning. What a feeling! I found out that other people really like ceremonies—even if they are "new," even if they have not been to India, even if they have not been around me and the work I do, and even if I do not think they are ready. They were in fact thrilled. I have never held myself back since.

That day, my body worker, Kerry, was feeling ill. I was extremely worried about her, but I had no time to rebirth her myself. I sent a fax to one of my teachers for help and told Kerry to stay in my room by the altar. At midnight Kerry ran to get me and my organizer. She was shouting that sacred ash was coming out of my picture of the Divine Mother! We ran into my room to the altar and sure enough, it was true. I told her to eat it. We all three ate it. She was instantly healed! The Mother was once again showing me her power. I was so glad I had a witness to these things and others could share the miracle.

The Mother is supreme reality. She is light itself. Transcendent. It is by her and through her that all things moving and motionless shine. It is by the light of her, the Divine, that all things manifest. A yogi told me this: "When everything else is stuck, only she is moving."

ANOTHER PAINTING

On that same tour, I went to Spain, where yet another mysterious occurrence happened out on the streets of Old Madrid. I love the way people stroll on the streets in Spain, rather than rushing around. Kerry and I were walking toward the place where I was to hold a women's group that night. The organizers had arranged it to be in an old palace. I was going to check the place out. There were mobs of people walking leisurely and so sweetly. I always feel that part of that sweetness is because they worship the Virgin.

Suddenly, I said to Kerry, "Look at that man over there with the crystal blue eyes. It is almost like he has been crying for nine months." I had no idea why I said that, but to my huge surprise and amazement, he walked over toward us and started to speak to me in Spanish. I was definitely not used to being recognized on the streets of Old Madrid. He started to tell me that his wife was coming to my women's group that night and that he had been painting a painting of the Divine Mother, and did I want to have it displayed? (Here it was again, the paintings!) I said, "Of course, certainly," not knowing that the painting would be better than I could ever imagine. I asked him how long it took to create the painting. He said, "Nine months . . . and I cried every day!" The exact words I had said. Another miracle.

When I saw the painting, I started to cry, and so did

my assistants. It was museum quality—like an Indian version of the Divine Mother. I asked Kerry to do a special puja to it. All the women that night bowed to the altar and that painting before the event began. Afterward, when he came to pick it up, he showed me posters that had been made and laid them out on the pool table. He told me that when he took the painting to the poster maker, he found out that the poster maker's wife had a fatal illness. And when the poster maker began to work on the poster from the painting, his wife was mysteriously cured!

I lost track of this painter for a few years. I thought he was somewhere in Madrid, but I could not find his address. Once I was in Valencia, Spain, and he showed up. I confessed to him that I had left the poster by mistake in someone's apartment in Madrid. He said, "No problem, I have another one for you." Once again, the Divine Mother came to me. I made the mistake of mailing it back to the USA and guess what? It got lost again. I could not find the painter any more, but I kept my intention to get another one. Eleven years later, my assistant in Spain brought a copy to my seminar. She happened to have two copies! Now I finally have it hanging in my Rebirthing room.

MORE APPEARANCES OF THE VIRGIN

That same year, I also went to Ireland. I don't usually read newspapers, and I wouldn't have time on tours even if I wanted to. But the Irish are such good writers! I picked up a newspaper one day and opened it to a page at random. There was a tiny paragraph there that said there was a statue of the Virgin Mary in a tiny village and that the statue was shedding real tears from one eye and blood from the other eye. I told Patsy that we had to find that village after the seminar. She was up for the adventure, even though we had to drive a long way and it was not easy to find. The village was precious beyond one's imagination.

The statue's owner led us into her house, and she was so humble and so sweet that I was once again reduced to tears, even before I saw the statue. During the experience, I felt the same energy I had felt in the underground temple in India and the same energy I had felt in Medjugorje, Yugoslavia. I was starting to really recognize this energy, to absorb it, and to long for it. Well, the point of all these stories is this: If you focus on the Goddess Divine Mother, she does begin to notice you and take you under her wing.

All this inspired me to want to visit the sites of the Virgin's appearances. I found a video about all the places the Virgin had been appearing in the world. I decided that I would go to Garabundal, Spain for the following Easter.

A BATTLE OF THE SEXES

After these abundant miracles, I tried to explain to my staff in a meeting that now the group's operations should be under the Divine Mother. The men got blocked. Nobody could breathe in the midst of that energy, and the business came crashing down. I kept trying to explain that this did not mean that I was taking the work back to the matriarchy . . . that would not even be allowed. But the energy still got stuck. During that meeting the cat started vomiting, and I was in a heap of tears.

It seemed as though I lost everything that year. But what I lost were entanglements. What I lost were the co-dependent parts of my business and the corrupt parts that I had denied even existed—the greedy aspects, the seductive power trips, and the unfair financial setups I did not recognize. I had ignored aspects, such as competition and the dysfunctional family patterns that we had all projected onto the business structure, which I had not been able to handle. I had also given my power away to the men in my own organization. This seeming disaster occurred right before I was to do the first ever Divine Mother Conference, in 1986. To be fair, I must say that some of the men later apologized to me and have surrendered since to the Mother.

For the first Divine Mother Conference, I had asked

Beth Hin and Leslie Temple Thurston to help me teach it. I knew it would be powerful, and I knew we would crack some real barriers. The outline for the event came to me in fifteen minutes in front of the Divine Mother murti in the Divine Mother Temple in Baca, Colorado, where Babaji devotees have created an ashram. When I read the outline to Beth and Leslie, they changed almost nothing. Only one suggestion was added. We were on! However, in preparation for the event, we had to do a lot of prayers and meditations.

In one meeting we had with men present, we were trying to discuss some of our projects and get their feedback. These were acquaintances of Beth and Leslie. An intense battle of the sexes was waged. We refused to get up and eat until it was cleared away. That took hours. I saw the same thing happen there that had happened to my own group. We three women were blazing trails and despite resistance, we went forward.

I chose Bishop's Lodge in Santa Fe for the event. The conference room was overflowing with wonderful women from all over, including my own mother. I had decided to practice first with the women alone and to put the men in a different wing with a male trainer. The idea was that we would all join at the end for a fire ceremony. I would say it came off perfectly, but for some reason, it took me nine months to recover and integrate this experience. At the next conference, the men and women came together for longer periods. And, later, the men and women finally came together for the whole time.

I had started my new mission, yes, but I was going out into what felt like the *void*.

LETTING GO

I had some initiations where I was literally knocked over by the energy. For example, I was due to go to Egypt for 12:12 (December 12, a special cosmic day, according to astrologers) and teach. But so much energy came into my body I could not get up from my bed at Emily Goldman's home in Santa Fe. I did not understand what was happening to me, but I got a strange call from a clairvoyant in Puerto Rico who told me she was seeing a master with white robes laying flowers at my feet and that I was entering an initiation and must stay where I was. In twenty-five years, I had never canceled an event. I only missed one appearance when my sister died, and I had to send a replacement. My not going to Egypt turned out to be another miracle, as I was told that too many teachers were at the event in Egypt and the situation was not good. I felt lucky that I had seen Egypt before, and I would not therefore miss out.

When the *shakti* is awakened, all the past impressions and karmas come out. I did not sleep for twelve days. Emily would get up and sit with me by the fire. Sometimes I would get in her bed if I was afraid. Beth came over and told me I was going to have to open my heart at the level of Gandhi and it would be hard. I was aware that I had to let go and empty myself so I could be filled with the renewed life force of the Mother, but I was rather terrified.

There were some speaking and teaching engagements during this period that I had to do no matter what. Sometimes I sat on the floor of airports in order to be grounded. I always told the audiences the truth about why I had to sit down. Once I was teaching at a church in Oregon. After the event, a very mystical woman came to me in the receiving line and said she had seen Babaji sitting over my head! I said, "Thank God! What did he say to you?" She said, "He told me to tell you that you are becoming the cave and he is taking off the trousers." I knew what that meant. I was in my masculine side a lot, being so much on the road back then. Had I been too much in my feminine side those years, when the patriarchy was so intact, I might have gotten ill. Babaji was saying to me this was changing and it was safe. The cave is his ashram in Herakhan, India. It is also the home of the Divine Mother, and it is where he first appeared. It is where I go each year to begin anew.

During the next two years, I was in a continual process of purification. It was very difficult, but whenever I felt hopeless, I was able to connect with one of the female saints, such as Amma or Mother Meera in Germany. They supported me beyond measure.

Very soon I accepted Amma as my female master, and Babaji encouraged that. I recall now one very special moment with Amma in Dallas, Texas: She had been taking everyone in her arms daily for three days from about 5 PM to 2 or 3 AM straight through. She did not stop once to go to the bathroom or drink. We would sit in the long darshan line and slowly creep toward her, going deeper and deeper and deeper into meditation. Then she would finally pick each of us up like a baby, and she would shout mantras in our ear, while at the same time she would be answering questions from another line of people. It seemed impossible. Even though I was used to Babaji, I still remained in awe of her. It was just like being with Babaji in the feminine.

On the last night, we all went early, and we were assigned to a team of four. Each group of four was given equipment to make an altar. Then we were given flowers to offer to the altar. We did this while she chanted, and then the lights went down and she took us all to a very deep level. At the end of the whole thing, when it was 3 AM, she stood on the stage and went into a trance and turned blue like

Krishna. Then she showered rose petals on us all—buckets and buckets of rose petals.

I read later that she travels so much because, she says, she must open hearts everywhere. She says that we are so stuck in the left brain, which cuts everything in separate pieces like a scissors. So she is working on bringing unity and oneness—through the heart, not the mind. I recommend you see her whenever possible. Check her website (www.Amma.org) for her tours near your area.

During the period I have mentioned, I was being taken over by the mightiest forces of the Divine Mother, but my ego often got in the way and gave me fear. I was so grateful to be able to read Swami Muktananda's experiences that he had written, because he helped me to understand *kundalini*. He had spent a quarter of a century in his direct search for God. The book I like best is *Kundalini: The Secret of Life*. I read a lot of books on kundalini which helped me, but most were written by men. Well, that is why I was instructed to write the next section.

According to the Hopis: "Man is created perfect in the image of his Creator. Then, after closing the door (at the top of the head) and falling from grace into the uninhibited expression of his own human will, he begins his slow climb back upward." Every time I would block this process, I would get really stuck, and when I would let go, there would be a miracle. *A Course in Miracles*, the series of spiritual lessons from the Foundation for Inner Peace, says that miracles are ordinary and that when they do not occur, something has gone wrong. Well, what has gone wrong, of course, is we indulged in our ego. But the ego is not really real, so everything is really a miracle. It is even a miracle that we have free will and we can think our own thoughts. But are our thoughts cooperating with God? That is always the issue. We have to give up our ego's thoughts.

It seems like the law of karma is just too big to handle by ourselves. We need the Divine Mother. We always have that choice of worshipping the Maya (the illusion), which is superficial, or worshipping the Mother, which is very deep. There is a good reason why they say in India, "Nothing is higher than worship of the Divine Mother." It is because she is beyond everything and behind all things. We must make it our quest to call the Goddess to us and invite her to teach us about life.

So to her, with great respect, we must bow and remember that *life* is a miracle. My own mother always told me this: "To be alive is a miracle."

THE DIVINE MOTHER AS KUNDALINI

Kundalini should be treated as the Mother herself. I once asked Ida Rolf, the founder of Rolfing, what the meaning of kundalini was. She said, "Oh, Sondra, only God understands *that*." She would not say another thing about it. I can see why now. It is something I hesitate to write about, because how does one adequately write about the prime creator? It is impossible. I can only share my experience of kundalini as I have been changed by it. All these experiences in this book happened to me after my masters opened my kundalini. I had my kundalini monitored by them and still do, or else I could not stand the might of it.

I can refer you to other books for your study:

1. *Kundalini: Transcendence of Psychosis*, by Dr. Lee Sanella

2. *Energies of Transformation: A Guide to the Kundalini Process*, by Bonnie L. Greenwell

3. *Kundalini, Evolution, and Enlightenment*, edited by John Warren White

4. *Kundalini: The Secret of Life*, by Swami Muktananda

5. *Living with Kundalini*, by Gopi Krishna

Muktananda says that the experience of kundalini is the true rebirth, where one is catapulted into a new world. He states that its unfolding has produced the great mystics and men of genius in every age. He makes it very clear that only a true guru can and should activate your kundalini. I could not agree more. Imagine someone's kundalini inadvertently opened by drugs. Things could go completely haywire fast. Some books even claim that this was the problem with Hitler.

In the chapter "The Nature of Kundalini," Muktananda talks about how every tradition speaks of kundalini in its own way: "In Japanese it is called Ki, in Chinese, it is called Chi, in Christianity, it is called the Holy Spirit. Whatever it is called, it is the Power of Consciousness. It is supreme energy whom the sages of India worship as the Divine Mother."

This supreme energy moves all creatures, so it makes everything work. The outer aspect of kundalini is therefore all pervasive. But until the inner aspect in a person is awakened, one never realizes one's true identity. Muktananda goes on to say that this kundalini shakti can be awakened by intense devotion to God, through repetition of the mantra, and, though rarely, spontaneously from past lives. But the easiest and best method is from the guru who transmits his power into the disciple. And only that guru can do it who has received it from his own guru and to whom kundalini has fully unfolded. This can be done by touch, word, look, thought, or by means of the mantra. I highly recommend you study his book carefully.

In my own case, I consider myself very fortunate to have a guru, Babaji. I consider Amma also to be my guru, and Jesus via *A Course in Miracles*. I was lucky enough to have my kundalini further awakened by Shastriji when I was ready. He told me he was my guru for seven lifetimes, and I was very happy to surrender to him since he was Babaji's high priest. He would put a tourniquet on my left arm and shout mantras in my third eye. I had no idea what it all was, but I bowed to him in gratefulness. The next year he would do my right arm and the following year both arms. It brought up all my past lives, which needed to be cleared. If you don't have a master, your kundalini could awaken but go to sleep again. If you have the grace of a perfect master, you can go all the way.

When the elements are purified enough in a person, the kundalini shakti has a free path to move through the chakras. It cleans you out! Your old personality goes out. Jesus said we must be born again. You can be given a new birth by the guru. The guru first destroys you and then recreates you. This is what Jesus does now, ever so carefully in *A Course in Miracles*. And that is why the books should and must be read according to the way they instruct. Don't jump around.

The true gurus want to give you their essence and their shakti. They want to give us everything. But the nervous system has to be ready. You have to build up to it. I did years of Rebirthing, Rolfing, and the Network Spinal Analysis along with spiritual practices. I also craved the destruction of my limitations and prayed for liberation. I am now learning that the greater my devotion to the Divine Mother, the faster my progress. As I said, the law of karma is too big to manage by ourselves. To handle it, always try to sit in the lap of the Divine Mother.

Sri Aurobindo, the great Indian saint who so often wrote about the Divine Mother, encouraged people to advance. He even talked about overcoming death. He called it the Yoga for Heroes to even try to conquer death. In other words, you are a hero for trying it. And the Bible said that death was the last enemy to overcome. You have to become a first-class warrior. Sri Aurobindo is the one who said, "Surrender to the Mother is the final stage of perfection." I visited his ashram in India and I got a lovely picture of The Mother who was at his side. Even back then, before Gandhi, she was saying that physical immortality was possible. She went further than most in her search.

It is very good to know that you can be given a new life. The energy can be awakened in everyone. Muktananda said, "There is no such thing as giving it to one and denying it to another. If one asks to whom the sun gives heat, the answer is to whoever stands in front of it."

According to Gopi Krishna, the awakening of the kundalini signifies a sudden or gradual change in the whole function of the brain. This involves the activation of a normally dormant area, which adds another channel of perception to the already existing senses. The eminent yogis of yore describe the phenomenon in hymns to the Goddess. They sing of the utter helplessness of the devotee and his entire dependence on the mercy and grace of the cosmic vital energy, Shakti, when the kundalini is aroused. As the mistress of the body, she and she alone is considered to be competent to bestow on earnest devotees the much coveted and hard to attain boon (blessing) of transcendental knowledge and supernormal psychic powers. Her devotees worship her with true loyalty—centering their thoughts and actions in her, resigning themselves to her will.

All these writings give kundalini the supreme position of being the queen and architect of the living organism—having the power to mold and transform it. There are many stories of common men and women who became the fortunate recipients of the grace of kundalini, and they soared to unrivaled heights of poetic and literary genius almost overnight.

He states the following: "The mechanism, known as

Kundalini, is the real cause of all genuine spiritual and psychic phenomenon, the biological basis of evolution and the development of personality, the secret origin of all esoteric doctrines, the master key to the unsolved mystery of creation, the inexhaustible source of philosophy, art and science; and the fountainhead of all religious faiths" (*Living with Kundalini*, p. 257). Now *that* is really profound. The author was certainly making a plea for scientific research to be done, but this was not taken up until after he died. He foresaw an era to come when more facts became known about this mighty power whereby a human could develop into a superbeing and become an inspiration suited to humanity's need for enlightenment. I think he would be pleased that there is now such a thing as a kundalini hotline! Although he was tormented by incredible suffering, due to the fact that he was unprepared for what happened to him, he still maintained he would go through it all again. (He himself could have used the kundalini hotline.) He always felt, until the end, that the awakening of the kundalini was the most wonderful achievement.

He completed his writing with this statement: "[Kundalini] provides the only method available to science to establish empirically the existence of life as an immortal, all intelligent power behind the physical phenomena on earth, and brings within its scope, the possibility of planned cultivation of genius in individuals not gifted with it at birth

. . . thus providing us channels for the acceleration of progress" (p. 381).

For more information, contact the Kundalini Research Foundation at http://www.kundaliniresearch.org/index.php.

TANTRIC SEX

No discussion of kundalini makes sense without including the subject of tantric sex. Tantric sex is worship of the Divine Mother. However, be forewarned that it is not advised to mess with Tantra without the guidance of a master, because the inner kundalini can rise. Ancient Indian texts criticize tantric sex as some Westerners present it. They say it is superficial and could be dangerous if you do not know what you are doing.

Even if you are not ready for tantric sex, why not start learning about it? I asked God once for the highest thought on relationships and sex. Within four days, someone came to the Theta House (where we started Rebirthing) and gave me a book on tantric sex. It was called *New Age Tantra Yoga*, by Howard Zitko. I read it four times. I was especially amazed that he related it to physical immortality!

In *Aghora: At the Left Hand of God*, Robert Svoboda says: "The merely curious have no business dabbling in Tantra. Tantric rituals are sacrificial rites. The sacrifice is on one's limited self. One should never practice classical Tantra without a guru. Ordinary sex is no sacrifice. When people come together to copulate, they usually seek gratification for themselves . . . the slaking of lust. Perhaps indirectly they satisfy their partners. Real Tantric Sex becomes possible only when one has totally effaced one's personality" (p. 16).

I should explain that there is the word *Tantra* and then there is *tantric sex*. Tantra in itself is a mental science. It is a method of exploring the mind, and it is worship of the Mother. One significant area of tantric research has always been learning methods of prolonging one's life. Even if one does not make it as an immortal, the tantric practices help one accumulate energy (shakti). Immortality is considered a desirable goal in Tantra. And tantric sex, when done correctly, can lead to physical immortality. Reading the books about this is one thing. Finding an equal who is willing to practice those rituals with you and handle the energy is another thing! Good luck!

The true aim of tantric sex is achieving union with the Divine. Even if you feel you are not ready for tantric sex, you could at least make sure you have an exalted view of the sex act. You can start by making the room where you have sex like a temple. Get the trash out of your bedroom. Get the office supplies out. Get out everything that is "stale." Make it holy. In this way, you can make sex more like a ceremony.

In tantric sex, frantic body motions and gymnastic contortions are eliminated. The focus is not on performance. The focus is on sharing love. It is not goal oriented. (Lasting energy is generated from stillness.) You are doing the sex ritual, and you are listening to space. This power can energize you for weeks. But to have this kind of sexual rebirth, you need to feel totally innocent and you need to understand that your body is divine. If you have been suppressed sexually by the church, by society, or by your family, you have to clear this and reconnect sex to spirituality.

Whatever path you choose, you do have to be disciplined enough to lift your consciousness to a place where the teachers can help you. You have to be open like a child. Open people are not rigid. You have to have broad views and constantly be willing to give up positions. I am always suggesting that you search for the highest. In your spiritual life, this is called the principle of right association, that is, placing yourself in the presence of those who force you to adapt upward. The reward of the path of the Divine Mother is bliss, knowledge, and much more!

With the avatar, everything is possible. You can become a channel for the power of the avatar, but it takes great purity. Gandhi himself said, "You have to be humbler than the dust." To be so humble, you have to be willing to weaken your ego continuously. I consider myself lucky to have one of the great avatars of the world: Babaji. Babaji has selected people from every stratum and every profession of life and is giving them various types of training. Each person gets a different type of training depending on his caliber and nature. The treatment is very different from what one is accustomed to. Tantric sex is very different from what one is accustomed to.

Watch out! Every facet of your existence will be changed, not just sex.

TRUE POWER AND THE DANGERS
OF FALSE POWER AND SEDUCTION

Meher Baba (the great guru who lived in silence for more than twenty years!) made the following statement in his writings: "As one accumulates power, the ego will balloon out, unless the ego personality is continuously incinerated simultaneously." This statement is one of the more important things I have ever read. You can understand the meaning of it if you look at some politicians or CEOs. People seem to want power; they crave it. Maybe this is because it feels like an aphrodisiac. But, of course, it is like playing with fire. In the Eckankar spiritual path, they say the greater you become, the quicker your acts come back to you. I certainly can vouch for this, being a public figure! Not only what you sow, shall you reap, but you shall reap faster. Along with power comes a huge responsibility and the danger of accruing a lot of karma fast.

True (spiritual) power is love, safety, and certainty. To be safe you have to be pure and free of anger and all those nooses mentioned earlier. To be certain you have to know that you are one with God and that you create your own results. You know what false power is. You see it all the time in the news.

One of my jobs is to communicate to the West what I learn in the East. In India, they have some very good practices. If a businessman gets a lot of money, he often will build a temple for the country immediately, and he will reach out with more community service right away to keep himself in check. *That* is a good idea. I wish rich people in the United States would help me build Divine Mother temples here! One can make a lot of money fast here, but one can get greedy just as fast. We see on TV everyday the dangers of the misuse of power. In my leadership seminars, I see very gifted people who are absolutely afraid of their power, because of some kind of memory they have of misusing power in other lifetimes. The consequences were too devastating. We do intense work on this so that they are able to come out again and be who they really are.

If one is not open to feedback and criticism, it is dangerous to have power because one can be going way off track without even being aware of it. Power trips on your own are very dangerous. Look at the cults. For this reason I wrote an essay in my book *Pure Joy* on the difference between a cult and a true spiritual family.

I have seen a lot of people who are afraid to give up their anger because they are afraid to lose "power." This is wrong thinking. This is ego. This is dangerous.

My guru Amma says, "Anger makes you weak in every cell of your body." A great being works very hard to become devoid of anger. It is not only dangerous to your body, but it is also not healthy for others. Anger provokes separation. Getting people to do what you want by using anger is bad karma. They do what you want or what the leader wants because they are afraid not to: Afraid of violence. Afraid of being damaged. Afraid of being thrown out. Afraid of being left. That is ruling by fear and is not true leadership. That is absolutely not right. Not in government, not in business, not it relationships. Our highest self knows this!

NEW PARADIGMS

That is exactly why we need the Divine Mother energy to teach us the new way. We need new paradigms. The old paradigms simply will not work much longer anyway. They are falling apart and will fall apart. Give it up! Get on the bandwagon. Ride the horse in the direction that it is going. Don't be part of the problem. Be part of the solution. I assure you that you do not want the karma of doing it the old way. If you are stuck in control and domination as a power trip, I suggest you stop this now and repent quickly.

You can study the great leaders in history and learn about all this. Watch the movie *Gandhi* over and over and over until you get it. A leader who knows what true power is can walk in the room and everyone surrenders. Once I was leading a large seminar on the island of Kauai on the subject of physical immortality. Five hundred students were there, and that was all the ballroom would hold. I begged my kahuna friend Al Kalakaua to come over from Maui to open the event. He got on the stage and said nothing. All five hundred people started crying. That is power; that is real spiritual power.

Many times I ran into the Saint Swami Satchinanda in airports, in hotels, and even once in a toy store. I would always break down crying just at the sight of him. Like Al Kalakaua, he exemplifies true power.

Mother Teresa said politicians should spend more time on their knees. Of course she was right, and we all know it. All this stuff about power is not just for political leaders. It is for any leader, any boss, any supervisor, and any parent. Are you a tyrant as a partner? Surely that will come back to haunt you, and I don't even need to tell you the results I have seen in Rebirthing clients. What suffering!

If you do not get how serious this is, you should surely read the book *God Speaks*, by Meher Baba. Anyone who can maintain over twenty years of silence in meditation knows what he is talking about! He covers the planes of consciousness. There are huge risks in each plane, but he discusses how very tantalizing temptations occur as you go up the ladder. He talks about the fact that some planes are the most difficult to cross. He says that misuse of power leads to an enormous psychic crash of unimaginable magnitude. "If the soul yields to the overpowering temptations to put his powers to wrong use, the explosive forces thereby released bring about a complete disintegration of consciousness, subjecting it to a cataclysmic downfall from the heights to the very lowest depths of the rudimentary stone age" (p. 50). In other words, you have to go all the way back to the very be-ginning of evolution! Then you have to go through the long and laborious ascent all over again—through ages of evolution and reincarnation through numberless forms. Do you really want to do that? Repent now. Give it up. You know who you are.

There is one plane that Meher Baba discusses further, which cannot even be crossed with one's own efforts. It is impossible. The grace of the perfect master is absolutely essential.

You might ask how one can make sure the ego is simultaneously incinerated when one has a position of power.

The answer is spiritual practices. Being on a spiritual path is vital.

Power can also be misused for the satisfaction of lust. I have seen the problem of seduction ruin so many missions. It is really a big test. Of course sex is always one of the big tests and so is money. The only thing *A Course of Miracles* would say about sex is this: are you in the ego's thought system with it or are you in the Holy Spirit's thought system with it? If you don't know what that question means, it is time to start reading *A Course of Miracles*! It would say the same thing about money.

Spiritual teachers say that most people are not interested in experiencing anything other than food, sleep, and sex, no matter what they claim. Or, they want happiness in the form of money, possessions, and fame. Very few want true spirituality, they say. In the book *Power vs. Force*, David Hawkins states that "in regards to progression of consciousness, it is not common for individuals to move from one level to another during their lifetimes. The energy field which is calibrated for an individual at birth only increases, on the average about five points" (p. 81). I think that is really sad! What about you? Well, I acknowledge you because if you are reading this book, you must be wanting spirituality. I honor you. I know things are changing.

THE GOD RUSH

Once I was in a beauty salon that rarely had current magazines (so I don't know how many years back this was), but in the *Women's Wear Daily*, there was an article about "the God rush." Famous people were finally admitting that they were becoming very spiritual and it was finally safe in Hollywood to admit it. Being on a spiritual path was in fact the "in" thing, they said. Of course, that can be tricky. Some people try to imitate spirituality rather than go through the deep process necessary.

One has to walk the spiritual path properly. There is a whole book about this called *Spiritual Materialism*. It says, "We can deceive ourselves into thinking we are developing spiritually when instead we are strengthening our egocentricity through spiritual techniques." I have seen people merely mouth spirituality, but they were not doing any real spiritual practices that require discipline and change. The main point of any spiritual practice is to step out of the bureaucracy of the ego. This requires real involvement in the spiritual life, not just reading about it or talking about it. In the New Age movement, I found it too easy to be a narcissist. I got trapped many times and had to be corrected.

In regards to the "Gold Rush" money, it is a visible sign of the universal force. Therefore in its origin and true action, it belongs to the divine. I read somewhere that we should regard wealth simply as a power to be won back for the Divine Mother and place it all at her service.

In fact, we should look at all that we have and get as belonging to her. We should be good trustees of money for her. Doesn't it feel right to say, "All power and money belong to the Divine Mother"? I say that to my altar to the Divine Mother: All power and money belong to you, Mother. I truly think that the whole monetary system should be redone in this way. I wonder what it would be like. . . . There must be some money somewhere in the world with the Divine Mother printed on it!

EFFECTS OF THE DIVINE MOTHER
ON FAMILIES

The Divine Mother is the love principle. Therefore our primary work is in relationships. This is how we grow. All that exists are relationships. It does not matter if one is single or married and in a traditional family or not. We are all in the family of man. Hopefully, you are also in a spiritual family!

How do you get out of the trap of having a dysfunctional family? Since the Mother is the source of all knowledge, we can therefore appeal to her to help answer this question.

Take a minute to think about families in a place like Bali, where families worship together every single morning for two hours before going to work! Just imagine all family members sitting together facing each other and making beautiful offerings for the Divine Mother. What does that bring up for you? I am sure you can feel the sweetness, the tenderness, and the holiness of what it must be like and how that affects their day. You probably think such a thing would be impossible in the West. Well, remember what it says in the Bible: "All things are possible!" You could be the one in your family to get this started in some fashion. You probably will say you don't have time and that even if you did, the rest of the family would never do it with you. But in fact, if you tried a morning ritual and you saw how much better your day went, I think you would change your tune.

If you could establish such discipline, not only would your children have good habits for their future, but you would also be working on the benefits for future generations. In Bali, it is simply astonishing to see the results of these practices. There is an overwhelming sense of harmony. Generally, you don't see people fighting. You don't see poverty. You don't see crime. You don't see anger. You don't see overweight people. You don't see suffering. Instead, you see the grace of it all. To start with, you get intoxicated with the aromas of the exotic fruits and flowers and incense everywhere. Then you have to handle bliss—people bowing to you, people living on another dimension altogether. Every home is built around a temple, and then each family relates to seven temples that they use. And there is the final Divine Mother Temple on top of a mountain with the government right there. It makes total sense to me.

RELATIONSHIPS

There is so much written on family therapy and family sociology. I wrote on the topic myself in other books on relationships: *Loving Relationships I*, *Loving Relationships II*, and *Essays on Creating Sacred Relationships*. What I noticed in all my travels around the globe is that there seems to be more sweetness in countries where they worship the Virgin or their version of the Divine Mother. There seems to be more bonding with the mother of the family herself, in those cultures. So I wonder, does this not also make for more peace? After all, in general women intuitively want peace because of the womb and the mothering aspect.

The thing that always amazes me about India is the fact that arranged marriages still go on there and there is so little divorce compared to the West. I have been studying and investigating this, because I could never imagine accepting an arranged marriage. This has always been fascinating to me. Well, I thought, Indian people are just plain more tolerant. We don't seem to be that way as much. Maybe we need to meditate on tolerance as a virtue.

Only recently it was explained to me that one of the big factors involved in the success rate of arranged marriages is the fact that the astrological charts of the potential couple are always done very carefully to make sure it is a good match. So the parents choose a mate for their offspring according to the matching up of these astrology charts and, of course, other factors. Then I thought, well, one could really encourage that in the West also, even though there are no arranged marriages. There certainly are enough astrologers in the United States and Europe today. However, would a couple really pay attention to this? If they were basing their potential marriage on the great sex they were having (as is often the case), they probably would not even listen to an astrologer who said their charts were not well matched. Would I? Well in my earlier years when I was rebelling, the answer would be no.

In my later years I did check this out. Once a teacher encouraged me not to have sex for nine months with a man I was in love with. She said that in the mystic schools, that was a test you were given. I decided to try it. I was really glad I listened to her. During those nine months I observed this man, and I got a red flag. I broke up with him, and I was glad I was not hooked on him sexually. On another occasion, I did ask a potential mate if he would mind having our astrology checked, and he agreed. It was not a good match, and we decided to be just friends. Many people might think that this would take the spontaneity out of a relationship. But if you are considering marriage, you must keep in mind that it is for the long haul. Nowadays, with the divorce rate so high, you should be very scrutinizing.

Divorce is devastating for most people. Keep in mind that even if you are awarded good child support, you might have trouble collecting it. According to some estimates, only about half of divorced men fulfill their child support agreements. I was pretty shocked to read this. If you are a man like that, I should think you would need to reconsider the karma of that.

Of course one can really grow from a divorce, and in my case there would never have been the gifts of my Loving Relationships Training classes and my research had I not been divorced. The original research I did as a rebirther was on how your birth trauma affects your relationships. After that, I continued to study how many other factors affect relationships such as the unconscious death urge, family patterns, past lives, and so on. Still, most people who get married hope they are not a statistic, and they want the family to thrive. However, you find out that Harvel Hendrix is right when he says that the unconscious purpose of marriage is to work out your childhood. Ultimately, you have to go through that. And you end up realizing that it is very important to have some spiritual purification techniques such as Rebirthing under your belt to handle all that.

All I know is that we better all pray a lot to the Divine Mother to learn how to handle relationships, marriage, and family nowadays!

GIVING BIRTH

When you think about families, you also have to start thinking about birth. For decades now, I have been researching the effects of birth trauma on humans and society and how to prevent that. But perhaps here it is also important to emphasize the absolute shamanistic aspect of a woman giving birth. It is said that a woman giving birth stands between the gateway of death and life, while she reaches over to bring through another soul. An African proverb goes like this: "Woman is like God, because she gives birth to the people." Anyone who meditates on this will surely have a renewed respect for women and mothers! In India, the question is posed: If you looked at all women as your mother, would you ever think of raping or cheating or deceiving one? Of course some people do not appreciate their mothers because they don't even appreciate life. I feel sad for them.

In times gone by, birth was much more ceremonial. There was music, midwives, and priestesses. . . . What happened? Why did it turn into something that is done in a male-dominated context of a hospital, where the doctor decides what the birthing process will involve? Women need to reclaim their bodies and decide how they want their babies to be born.

I wrote a book called *Ideal Birth* at the feet of my guru

in India. It is about underwater birth! There are now so
many important books to read on the subject:

1. *The Secret Life of the Unborn Child*, by Thomas Verny

2. *Birth without Violence*, by Frederick Leboyer

3. *Birth Reborn*, by Dr. Michel Odont (This was written by
   an obstetrician who recommends throwing out the delivery table.)

These books should not be taken lightly. They are
major works and should be given as presents to any woman
you know who is even thinking of getting pregnant so she
can read it even before delivery. Or if you know someone
who is pregnant, never hesitate to give these books as a gift.

I have been present at underwater births in Russia and
America. I have been watching these babies who were born
underwater grow up. I have had the pleasure of staying with
families for awhile where there were "underwater babies" in
their family. The effect of one of these beings on the whole
family is mind blowing. I feel extremely privileged to have
these souls in my life. They are advanced, and they are
teachers. If you read *Ideal Birth* and the above-mentioned
books, you will see why babies born with reduced birth
trauma are so advanced. They are able to retain their connection to the Divine Mother so much more easily, for one

thing. Remember, in India, they say that the Divine Mother is the foundation of all of one's capabilities and the source of all knowledge.

THE SHAKTI OF CHILDREN

Children are connected to the source of everything, and this is precisely why children are so wonderfully awesome. Unfortunately, as we grow up, so many things make us shut down: birth trauma, suppression in school and church, etc. Those children who have less birth trauma are able to remain more connected to the Divine. This is our constant experience as rebirthers.

All great teachers repeatedly say that adults should listen to the children. Children are able to channel from the divine very easily. They will often have the highest thoughts of family members for this reason—if only the family would listen. Children, however, will also act out the unconscious minds of the parents. This drives parents nuts because they do not want to see their own shadows. But the truth is this: children are the gurus in the family. That means they will teach the adults what they are suppressing, and at the same time, they will channel high thoughts from the Divine. In families where this is understood, there is a totally different energy. Think the opposite of suppression. It is exciting!

However, some parents cannot stand that much excitement because they were not allowed to have that much fun when they were kids. So they try to stop the aliveness and fun in their own children. What a pity. People deny themselves excitement by suppressing the children. Of course it is quite confrontational to realize that your child is acting out your subconscious mind.

The founder of Rebirthing, Leonard Orr, taught me the following: Love takes upon itself your negatives so you can see them more clearly. So children, out of love, are showing you what might hurt you from your own mind. This profound statement is something that everyone in a family should understand. In families, everyone is always acting out each other's "case" (suppressed material limitations, negativity, ego, patterns, birth traumas, death urges, past lives, etc.). If family members do not have a clue that this is going on, things can be extremely difficult. You want to get out, escape, rebel, and often things get so bad that the family unit breaks down or breaks up. In the end, some people go to the grave hating their parents. What a tragedy! If you knew that you chose your parents and you have karmic lessons to learn from each one, you might see it all differently. For example: What was your purpose for choosing that mother? That father?

In the Vedas, they say your mother is your first guru. Motherly love is perhaps one of the highest forms of love. A good mother can make all the difference in the world. I can now see the saintly aspect of my own mother. I had the good fortune of meeting the mother of Muniraj, one of my gurus, in India. His mother was astonishingly holy, so much so that I find myself bowing to my computer in her honor as I think of her right now.

Once I did a seminar for children in Valencia, Spain. Sixteen children came, and they ranged in age from two to ten years old. I placed them in a circle with their parents in the room. I began by asking each one what they like about life. Mostly they commented about animals and nature. Then I asked them if there was anything they did not like about their home. They thought I meant about the physical space so they all said that was okay. But when I changed the wording and asked them if there was anything they did not like about their family, they really spoke up! They said they did not like the wars going on in their families. They did not like the fights. They wanted peace. They also said they wanted their parents to know that they *were* love! I was really stunned. They had so much energy that I had them perform. One girl got up and sang a song. She was only five. That was the only thing that made them quiet. They all became quiet and showed her so much appreciation. They seemed to know she was in her higher self. Even the little tots were quiet. Amazing.

The energy got so high that I had to go lie down and breathe after all this. Can you handle the shakti of your own child? If you allow it in, you will be healed. Miracles can occur. But you might have to breathe a lot. Maybe one or more of your children has tremendous *light*. Don't suppress the light—this has been called the Herod factor. Be prepared to let your children become masters. The children coming in now are very high beings. They have come to repair us and teach us joy. Overdisciplining, dominating, and controlling them does not make sense.

Allowing them to be who they are and setting a good example gives them breathing room. That does not mean that they take over either. You are their guides, giving them framework. Pray for the right balance.

One of my teachers stood in front of my mother once and acknowledged her as a great mother. He said to her, "You allowed Sondra to be different, and we all benefit from that." He was right about her. She gave me space and she set a framework of holiness and integrity, and so I did not want to disappoint her. This space inspired me to be good.

One thing I did not cover enough in my earlier books was how past lives can affect a family. I would now like to refer people to the wonderful book by Dr. Roger Woolger called *Other Lives, Other Selves*. One should take it all in like a serious study. There is also a chapter in the book *Star Signs*, by Linda Goodman, called "Déjà Vu." She gives an example how in one lifetime, John hurts Mary; then in the next lifetime they reincarnate, and Mary hurts John. And in the next lifetime, John hurts Mary; and in the following lifetime, Mary hurts John. And they go through umpteen dreary lifetimes until in one lifetime, one of them decides to forgive and break the chain. There is another book to read by Dick Surpton called *We Were Born Again to Be Together*. Check it all out.

Of course when I grew up, this topic of past lives did not even exist in our community or church. It was also kind of a taboo subject with my mother as it seemed against religion. Now I see that it is why we were all stuck in our family! Often you have very intense past lives with your blood family, especially siblings, for example. The biggest regret I have is that I could not work out my relationship with my sister before she died. She died in her early fifties, and for ten years after her death, I was working on that. I could never understand why our relationship was so impossible until I had our past lives checked out.

Recently I moved back to California. When I arrived at a friend's apartment, I met the neighbor across the hall. I commented on what a cute baby she had. She did not know me from Adam, but she replied, "Yes, he was my grandfather, and he has reincarnated," not batting an eye. It felt right and I remember thinking, well, here I am, back in California.

It is interesting to think of what a family could be like. In my case, my mother had to work all the time, as my father was sick all the time. These were great people, my parents, but it all felt like a tragedy. At meals when we were finally all together, I wanted to get away quickly because my father took so many pills. We went to church, but my parents never seemed to have the same religious fervor at the same time. At first my dad was really into it, but then as he got sick, he disconnected from it and my mother got really into it. And anyway, we would just sit and stare at the patriarchal minister. It was never any fun.

Think about Bali where families are making offerings together each day. Think about them going to the temples together and bowing together to the Divine Mother and the ongoing bliss. Feeling the difference has made me want to write a chapter on Bali (see chapter 6).

There is an absolutely beautiful book called *The Heart of the Goddess*, by Hallie Iglehart Austen. In the introduction, she states the following: "Research from every continent indicates that from roughly 30,000 to 3000 BC, women and the Goddesses were honored. Most of these cultures were highly developed technologically and artistically, and some existed in peace for at least one thousand years. Women and men lived in partnership rather than domination." On page 20, she gives a beautiful meditation where you can imagine a culture that is peaceful for a thousand years, having a heritage without war, draft, or military taxes.

What would it be like if our society's resources were

focused on sustaining and rejoicing in life? Imagine living in harmony with other forms of life. Austen's book contains images of the Goddess from all over the world. The knowledge of the Goddess, she says, has been lost and obscured by patriarchal repression and distortion. Blaming men is not the point. We all cocreated that. Some of us women were men in those past lives who repressed women. The point is to reawaken and imagine what family life would really be like if we honored the Goddess and the sacred feminine.

Since the Mother bestows worldly and spiritual blessings, why would you want to keep her out? Invoking the Divine Mother will bring more life to your family—more union, more abundance, more cooperation and peace, more health, more joy, more spiritual power, and more creativity. What are you waiting for?

FIVE MEN WHO HAVE SURRENDERED TO THE DIVINE MOTHER

I am aware that men may wonder about the value of surrendering to the Divine Mother, so I decided to interview a few men who I knew had done this. Even though some would call them "yogis," they do not live in ashrams permanently. They have normal lives, children, and successful businesses.

Rai Dass (German)

I interviewed Rai Dass and the following are his words.

What surrender to the Divine Mother means is giving the woman inside yourself an adequate place, because the worship only starts always on the inside. But the aim is to awaken the corresponding part in ourselves.

In our time (in women as much as in men) this male power is so predominant that the worship of the Mother is a very important thing. When you discover the Mother inside of you, life will become much easier because you do not have to always run. You don't have that kind of pressure: 'I am the doer. . . . I have to do.' When the receptive (let it happen character) comes through, our life gets much more relaxed. And on the other hand, this caring quality for beings around us, and for our own being, gets uplifted and stronger in us.

I am talking about the Goddess with each of us. The closer you get to her, the less important it is if one is talking about male or female. In the end, there is only *her*. You know Jesus was very balanced. The Mother part in him was very strong. So then, if we are talking about the Goddess within each of us, why do we need outside worship of the Deity as you see her? These outside pujas are a help (through visible expressions of love) to slowly get in contact with that invisible one living in the heart. Doing the pujas teaches us to love. Through the mixture of offerings and mantras, we call the Divine inside us and create a concentration of energy, which is extremely helpful for transformation.

Through her grace, our demons are conquered. There is the symbolism of her conquering demons. The demons represent our bondage. Those demons keep us from realizing the Divine in ourselves. She takes away our ignorance . . . such as habitually being stuck in likes and dislikes, or endless desires (I want, I want, I want,), and the "I Mine" attachment. By getting more and more out of these bonds, you become one . . . like a drop in the ocean.

At the end of this interview, Rai Dass sang "*Amba Amba Jay Jagadamba*" (Praise to Amba, Mother of the Universe . . . all forms are one).

Harigovind (Swiss)

Harigovind wrote this at my request on an ordinary typewriter many years ago in my flat in Seattle. But then he tore it up into many tiny pieces because he did not think it was good enough. "How can one ever write well enough about the Divine Mother?" he asked me.

During the night I went down to the wastebasket and took out all the little pieces and pasted them together. I still think what he wrote is absolutely divine. Here it is:

A very dear friend of mine was crossing Germany by foot during the Second World War. One day she found herself in the situation where a Russian soldier entered the room in which she had taken shelter. He was ready to rape her. Instead of going into fear and terror, she stood calmly, sending her prayers to the Divine Mother. The soldier stood immobilized for awhile. Then he suddenly sank down to his knees and burst into tears and begged her forgiveness. What happened? Remembering the Mother changed his entire behavior. Perhaps he also remembered his own mother.

We must not only recognize God in the father form, or only in the form of the mother of God as Mary. We must come to recognize the Divine Mother herself in all her forms.

The Divine Mother unifies and diversifies. She is the one in the unfolded universe and the universe is one in her. She is the one substance which is the substratum of every communication, of every creation, of every display of power and beauty. She is the one every artist strives for as the transcendent expression of his art. She is the one every businessman strives for in his success; and is the one who shines in every human heart when in love. She is the one who perfects science, the Great Inspiratrix who gives the lift of knowledge to the minds of leading scientists. She is the origin of consciousness, of all the elements, of all the laws of physics, mathematics, music, economics, languages. She is the primordial cause of all existence, and is eternally one with Shiva, the simple Father.

To speak about her is courageous and perhaps foolish at the same time; because She can never be fully reached with words, yet She is the Mother of letters and language which She pervades. To write about the Divine Mother resembles the attempt to empty the ocean with a teacup. For She is Omnipotent, Omnipresent and Omniscient. In her the infinite potentiality is slumbering, to be evolved into the screens of time and space according to her Will.

The Mother is Supreme. She encompasses all opposites and transcends them all. She is supreme power, supreme wisdom, supreme peace, the supreme of the supreme. Name her electricity, name her gravity, name her space. We have learned to use them all, but can we create their existence? Can we create even the smallest flower of the most modest moss?

To have the blessing of her sight, the saints and scientists of all ages have undergone great penance. In order for the blindness of our inner eye to be lifted, we have to pray to her with the full power of our heart.

All mankind is striving for happiness . . . but lasting happiness can be found only in true knowledge, and true knowledge implies the knowledge of the Divine Mother. The "Father oriented" Western mind has created the technological civilizations to be highly developed. But the feeling side, the inner connection with the matrix, creatrix, the life-giving spring of inner certainty and intuition has nearly been lost. However, the skill to handle the scientific technological aspects of modern life has not been developed.

In the West, the absence of the Divine Mother in image and experience resulted in our orientation becoming lopsided and out of balance. There is no difficulty in seeing proof of that in the massive threat of nuclear war, pollution, and destruction of our forests. The real solution to all these problems can lie only in a shift of consciousness, in a reorientation of the mind in the same manner as the Russian soldier woke up from his dream. A new orientation to the Divine Mother's energy, a tuning in to a higher wisdom is needed. It can be revealed to us through prayer and meditation, as we are all children of the one Mother.

O Mother of Bliss, Thou fillest me with supreme joy. Thy mercy is boundless, O Mother, forever I bow to thee. Teach me. Teach me how to be more loving, teach me how to be a caretaker of this planet.

Jai Mahamaya Ki Jai! *(Hail to the Great Universal Creative Energy)*

Can you believe he threw this away?

Kailua (Italian)

Kailua told me he tried to understand the Divine Mother by worship of the *dhuni* (sacred fire temple). He said that through the fire, with time, you start to understand something. You also get the *darshan* (blessing presence) of the Divine Mother. He told me that Babaji taught him to worship the fire (the Divine Mother), as this is an ancient Vedic ritual. Before he did this, he had three years of preparation as the *pujari* in the Italian temple. Then he went to the fire temple. He felt such a responsibility that for him it was like

79

taking care of a child. Everyday he would get up at 3:30 AM to prepare for the fire ceremonies.

He told me that there was no meditation without the dhuni and no knowledge without the dhuni. He explained how just sitting close to the fire puts the mind at peace. He understood the fire as an element, not something to burn up garbage. However, the fire will burn up the rubbish of the mind, he pointed out. Bad things burn out, and the beauty of the person comes out instead. Fire purification is an ancient practice. He told me that before this practice he was hard with himself and others and very strict. Now he had become soft and more open. The fire had transformed him.

Krischen (American)

I met Krischen in Colorado. I was very struck by how enlightened he seemed for such a young man, so I interviewed him. He told me that the first book he ever read outside of school was *The Autobiography of a Yogi*, at age eleven! He became a yoga teacher and taught kundalini yoga and hatha yoga twice a week. But he had to work in a grocery store to make ends meet. His life was in pieces, not together at all. He had a lot of trouble getting rent money. One night he prayed so much he had this thought: Surely the greatest yogi somewhere could hear me. Then he had a dream. He was

suddenly sitting with a yogi by a fire pit, and he remembered seeing a mole on the neck of that yogi. He had no
thoughts whatsoever. The yogi became a guru and said the
following, "You can come and stay at my ashram at any
time." He saw people who were working for no reason. This
was another realm. He concluded that if you worked at
ashrams, you would enter those other realms.

Later he saw a picture of Muniraj (who now holds the
space for Babaji), and he realized that he was the one in
the dream. He decided to give up everything and go into the
woods. He looked at his map and realized that somehow he
had marked Willow Lake fourteen years earlier. He started
walking in the area at the end of Baca at Crestone, because
that is where a driver dumped him off. He hiked into the
woods. The second day he found a cave, and he started
doing kriya yoga inside it. Days later, he came down and
discovered there was in fact a temple below him! He went to
the *Aarti* (chanting service) and met the yogis.

He fell in love with the Divine Mother murti (activated statue) and felt that that was all he needed. He asked
her to help him grow up! This was the spark that changed
him. She put him through all the things to teach him, and
he got all that he wanted.

He finally met Muniraj, whom he had seen years before
in the dream, and when they met, Muniraj gave him a name.
Muniraj looked at him and pushed his lips together, and

Krischen knew he must go into silence. He went through such incredible changes that his friends could not believe it. All his desires were gone, but everything he needed came to him.

The main thing he understood is that the Divine Mother is the whole of creation. Everything is a feminine field. The murti is the magical equation of the Mother, he said—like the Ark of the Covenant. One night he saw the Mother dancing in the temple on another dimension. All his bad habits disappeared. All the chants turned into something magical, like the mantra chanting him.

You can visit this wonderful ashram in the United States by contacting Baca Ashram, PO Box 9, Crestone, CO 81131; 719-256-4108; hua@amigo.net.

About Shastriji, to Whom This Book Is Dedicated

It is my supreme honor to dedicate this book to Shastriji, whose entire life was in the devotion to the Divine Mother and whose entire life demonstrated the miracles of the Divine Mother. Recently he took samadhi (conscious departure) at the age of ninety-eight, during the most auspicious astrology of the Harmonic Concordance. He departed Nov. 19, 2003. A Vedic astrologer told me that at the time of his samadhi, Shastriji had the purest chart possible. Shastriji was, for one thing, Babaji's high priest. Babaji is the immortal maha avatar who is my master and whom Yogananda honored in *Autobiography of a Yogi*.) Babaji is the emanation of Divine Light. He is the power of the Eternal Father, Mother, and the Divine Child. He can assume any form he wishes—anywhere, anytime. He can change that form in the blink of an eye. He materialized a youthful body in 1970 and was accessible for fourteen years to us during his last visit.

Shastriji was the mouthpiece for Babaji. He was and still is, along with Muniraj, the pure essence of Babaji. (Muniraj, the guru currently in residence in Babaji's ashram in India, is called the king of sages. Babaji charged him with the task of continuing his work and mentioned further that Muniraj was an incarnation of Dattatreya, the first master, who was a combination of Brahma, Vishnu, and Shiva. He is our guru and you are welcome to come to India with me and meet him—see my website, www.sondraray.com.

Shastriji was and is, according to Babaji, one of the most learned men on Earth. (See his picture on the dedication page in the beginning of this book.) He was a saint and everything you imagine a saint to be. Furthermore, he was a Ayurevedic doctor, astrologer, palmist, pure clairvoyant, and especially a Sanskrit scholer. He has been a poet in all lifetimes. He has great wisdom of the Vedas and their rites and has been the interpreter of Indian myths and the Santana Dharma, as the

Indians call their original religion. His many books are a pure inspiration, all of them being in mantric verses.

His main work of historical content was a vision about Sri Babaji's incarnations through all times. He prophesized Babaji's incarnation as the lord of lords and world teacher. He has told me that his best work was the *Haidakhandi Sapta Sati*, seven hundred verses in praise of the Divine Mother. When he gave it to his first guru, his guru put the manuscript on his head and began dancing all around, saying, "I am an old crow and do not deserve this beautiful script, but when the swan will come, within your lifetime, then give it to him." (The swan was Babaji.)

During his discipleship with his guru, Mahedra Baba, Shastriji had received a profound preparation to recognize and serve the Lord (Babaji) in his fourteen-year sojourn on earth. In fact, he had written most of his works in mantric verse on Haidakhan Baba many years before Babaji's physical appearance in 1970. When asked, Shastriji emphasized that whatever he has written was "by the grace of my master and by direct inspiration of the Lord himself. I am merely a writing instrument."

One time Shastriji told me the story that when he was young, his guru Mahendra took him outside into the Ganges River during a certain astrological configuration, wrote a mantra on his tongue, and then hit him over the head with a stick! From that moment on writings began to pour out of him! Of the sixty-five books he has written, he says that the one dedicated to the Divine Mother is the most powerful.

Whenever Babaji gave his short informal talks at his ashram in Haidakhani, at the Himalayan foothills, Shastriji would be asked by him to repeat his every word, before they were translated into English. One month before his guru Mahendra Baba left his body, he said the following to Shastriji: "Brother Vishnu, if the Lord should appear during my absence, then this secret mantra will help you recognize him. This mantra is known only to the Lord and no one else. It is a mahamantra and was given to me by the Lord himself." As he spoke to Shastriji, the divine master smiled and touched his head three times with his lotus hand.

In February, 1971, Sri Haidakhan Bhagwan (Babaji) came to Vrindavan, and Shastriji was overcome when he heard word for word the same secret mantra from the Lord's own lips whispered into his ear! He said that his heart was filled with joy and his soul was immersed in a sea of bliss. His body was elated, and his voice failed him. Then the conviction dawned on him that Babaji was in fact the Ultimate Absolute Divine worshipped by his own beloved guru Mahendra. He turned around and announced the truth to the world.

Shastriji taught me that divine love is beyond everything. He seemed to always be in a constant state of prayer. To be near him was a miracle. His base of knowledge and caliber of being was and is unfathomable. His whole family was constantly demonstrating bliss as they took care of us. Miracles happened at his home frequently. He personally saved my life many times. To me, Shastriji absolutely demonstrated the results of the point that the Divine Mother is the foundation of all one's capabilities. I know he prayed to her for around five hours a day. He was and is a true child of the Divine Mother. That is what his whole life was about on earth. He told me he was my mother, my father, my husband, and my wife! In supreme gratitude to him, I offer up this book on the Divine Mother.

Following are some words from Babaji himself about Shastriji: "He is a true son of Mother Saraswati, the goddess of wisdom. It was she who sent him."

From "Words from Guru Gorakhnath through Sri Babaji," published in Germany, by Nila Renata Caddy: "He has been a poet in all lifetimes and a writer of many epics at many different times in history. He attained self realization through Kakbusbundi, a sage living permanently on a hill top in the Himalayas. He is the original poet saint and world teacher of all times. Such greatness is Shastriji."

Here is what Babaji himself said about the verses Shastriji has written:

The great power that is the Cosmic Maya, The Supreme Divine Energy, the Mother Goddess embodies the totality of all this is to be known, being the combined divine Grace Energy of the Goddess Mahakali. Mahalakshmi, and Maha-Saraswati. To worship the lotus feet of the Universal goddess in this form gives human life its highest realization.

The publication of the *Shri Haidakhand Sapta Sati* is a great blessing and boon, as it facilitates her worship. Every word of the great prayer is a divine mantra. Reading it and reciting it with proper dedication cures diseases, rids the mind of worries, and solve all problems, while this aspirant on the spiritual path attains the divine perfection he desires, prosperity in life, worldly happiness, and spiritual peace. Allow these prayers to make you happy. This is my wish and blessing to you.

It is my pleasure to have permission to share a few of Shastriji's verses here with you:

Thou are the Force Sublime, Exalted Wisdom
Absolute Boundless Peace, Beyond the Ultimate
Mother, Thou art above the reach of all qualities
Bramham Vishnu and Shiva bow to you

Thou takest the form of all abundance
All growth is under Thy command
Thou are the vigor of all living creatures
We honor Thee, O Benefactress of the World.

No one can ever dream to count
The Jewels at the bottom of the ocean
And even a gifted poet cannot describe
The brilliant splendor of the sun
In this way, Bliss-bestowing Mother of the Universe
Who in this world is able
To tell the tale of Thy Magnificence and Glory?

Out of affectionate love for those who love Thee
Thou givest Thy Holy Vision to their eye
Thou bringest forth a blissful stream of nectar
Which like the Holy Ganga
Cleanses the world of all sins.

And a verse from me to my guru:

To you, Shastriji, I bow, before your indescribably
Glory as a fount of all knowledge. May everything I
Write be something beautiful for God and to honor
You and the Divine Mother

6

BALI AND THE DIVINE MOTHER

I will tell you about one culture that is clear on who is running things, and that is Bali. The Divine Mother Temple rules. It is on a mountaintop, and the Balinese government officials live and work right there!

I have traveled around the world for decades, and never have I found anything as incredible and wonderful as Bali. I want to share some of the results I saw in a culture that has it together. I still cannot believe that the first time I went, I ended up alone in Bali for six amazing weeks. It was one of the best experiences of my life!

It all started when I came back from India with my head shaved after my second visit. I was wondering what it was going to be like to be a public figure in America with my head shaved for nine months. I was surprised how magnificent it all was, because I went into an altered state and stayed there most of that time! Of course, I had to rise above all the judgment of others. I got off the plane at Los Angeles, and my friends who came to meet me told me there was a new movie in town I had to see called *Altered States*. I thought this was very funny as I was already in an altered state! In the middle of the movie, when the characters came out of the deprivation tanks like animals, I went out of my body and I heard a voice. It was obviously Babaji talking to me. He said, "You must do the God Training. It is not a question of can you do it or will you do it. It must be done." I said, "Well, okay then."

I came crashing into my body wondering *what* I had committed to. I could not figure it out for one and a half years, and finally I could not stand it anymore. I told my staff I was leaving for Bali (the Island of the Gods) for an undetermined time to get clear on this.

A GUIDE APPEARS

It was a long flight, but the result was way beyond my imagination. I arrived in the dark, so I decided to stay at a well-known hotel the first night and splurge. It was the Oberoi. After all, I had met Mr. Oberoi himself in New Delhi and I was impressed. He was like the Hilton of the East to me. I think he then had twenty-six hotels. My bungalow had a sunken tub . . . simply beautiful. The next morning I breakfasted outdoors on a terrace by the beach. The Balinese waiters struck me as something like saints. They were always bowing to me. My first comment to God was, "Dear God, what has happened to the Western world? This is heaven."

But I had to find a cheaper place to stay, since I expected to stay a few weeks. So I started walking down a road looking around. A very nice, mature Balinese man on a motorcycle suddenly approached me saying "Madam, do you need a guide?" I said, "Oh definitely, how much?" He replied, "You pay me what you feel." I knew Babaji had sent me this wonderful man. He took me around, and I found a place at Poppies Cottages, walking distance to the beach. The most amazing thing was this: every day my guide would come from a long distance and bring me offerings for my altar that his family had made in the morning. He did this every single day for six solid weeks. Amazing!

That is when I was told that all families in Bali do puja (worship) together every morning. They may do this for two hours before work. They would never consider going to work without doing that. I was also told that every home has a temple in the middle of the home and that that temple was built first before anything else. Then I learned that each family relates to seven different temples. There is the indoor temple, the outdoor temple, the local town temple, the local district temple, and on and on until you finally get to the great Divine Mother Temple on the mountain, which is supreme. Not only that, but they actually use these temples. They are not relics sitting around. They are used constantly.

The day I finally made it to the main Divine Mother Temple, I was stunned while climbing up to it. What intrigued me the most was the fact that there was an open-air covered hall to the side of it with nothing inside—just a beautiful floor, pillars, and Balinese roof. I asked my guide, "What is this space for?" He told me that it was where the elder priests met to solve any problem that came up. I kept on thinking about that place for some reason, imaging them doing prayers and ceremonies there. But I did not see any problems in Bali to speak of.

Because of "Big William," my guide on the motorcycle, I got to see a lot of places in Bali that most tourists never see. I became convinced that Bali was from some other dimension somehow. The people were all beautiful. Everything was abundant. I saw no overweight people, no crime, no conflict. In fact, the people literally acted out their dramas and egos onstage in such a way that they did not have to do it in their daily life. Each village I visited mastered a certain trade. One village mastered batik. Another stoneware. Another silver. Another baskets. Another art. You can watch them do these crafts. All villages are cooperating with each other. But the main thing is that there are active altars everywhere at work.

When I finally attended a performance of Balinese dancing, my comment to God was, "These dancers have to be super advanced yogis. I see no other way they could do these movements and *mudras* (sacred positions of the hands)." Then I found out that a dancer is chosen very young and spends her whole life mastering that one dance to perfection. I would go into a trance watching. Or maybe they were in a trance, and I caught it. The men also put themselves into a trance by fire walking. This seemed to be how they "rebirthed" themselves, to use our term. Later, I did read in Barbara Marciniak's book that Bali is, in fact, descended from another dimension.

DRINKING THE DIVINE

I have never felt so good physically in my life as I did in Bali. Of course, it also had a lot to do with the fact that I was reading the *Course in Miracles* texts four hours a day and drinking mostly freshly squeezed juices from the exotic fruits of Bali, which they fix up for you in blenders at little *tienda*s (outdoor stores). I also liked the Balinese black rice pudding. Daily I would outline the text of *A Course of Miracles* for myself to try to understand it better. Later I was instructed to get the outline published. That is the book called *Drinking the Divine.* I felt as though I was always drinking the divine in Bali. I stayed to myself most of the time, but I never once felt lonely. Once a day I would walk to the beach, and there was always the opportunity to have two women massage you at once for something like four dollars. This daily nurturing was miraculous.

Sometimes I would take a horse-drawn carriage at night and just go into bliss. I was always inhaling the combination of very exotic aromas: the temple incense (which was everywhere due to so many open-air temples), the clove cigarettes, exotic fresh fruits hanging on the trees, and very beautiful flowers growing everywhere. The combination of these aromas was intoxicating. And at the same time there was also always beautiful temple music being played in the outdoor temples. I knew I had arrived in heaven. Try to imagine it. Better yet, think about going. Bali changed my life. As soon as I came home, I put an altar in every room, including the bathroom.

The people were always bowing to me. I have never felt so safe. One day I looked out my window, and I happened to see the most beautiful sight. There were one hundred women walking in a row, all dressed beautifully in batik. Each was carrying an elaborate huge headdress made of fruit and flowers. I could not believe that an apple or two was not falling off! I was immediately inspired to run after them to see where they were going. I was desperate to find out what was going on as they led me down to a remote beach. I searched and searched for someone who could speak English, and I finally found a lady from the embassy. She said to me, "Oh, you are so fortunate to be able to see this ceremony. This is the day they pray for families." Then people came out of their homes and laid down beautiful batik cloths all in a row along the beach. The women knelt down and took the fruit and flower arrangements off their heads and put them on the cloths on the beach. People kept coming in droves and knelt down and prayed on the beach all day for their families. I found out everyone on the whole island was doing that. This blew my mind for years. That was the day I surrendered to Bali.

That day, I received the knowledge of how to do the God Trainings that Babaji had asked me to do. It all came to me in fifteen minutes after the ceremony. So easy. So fabulous. Why, I asked myself, did it take me one and a half years of not getting it, and here I could get it so fast? I think the answer is obvious. The God Trainings became like a rotating ashram I started doing around the globe wherever I was instructed to do so, usually at different power spots: Mount Shasta, California, was the first one. Later we went to Egypt; Machu Picchu, Peru; Sedona, Arizona; and other places.

More Guides and Miracles

I experienced constant miracles in Bali. People would just show up and guide me to wherever I was supposed to go. One day I was sitting in Poppies Cottages Restaurant, reading the *Course in Miracles* text, as usual. A wonderful man with white hair approached me and told me he was Australian. He said that a clairvoyant had told him that he was going to run into me in Bali! It was his last day however, so he begged me to come to Perth and rebirth him and his friends. I told him that it would have to be another year, as I had just been called to India. Then he told me to be sure to go to Monkey Forest Road near Ubud, up in the Balinese hills and find this certain priest and experience his body-work. He also told me to go to a specific restaurant and order the dish number 14.

The next day I was in a van going up into the mountains to Ubud, the artists colony, where I soon found Monkey Forest Road. The monkey forest was remarkable, but the priest was even more amazing. After bathing, he came out in white robes and began to prepare for my session. He poured something into my ears that was rather like the white lightning that is drunk in the southern states. He drank some himself, and then he started walking on my back. He seemed to know intuitively every form of body work I had ever had in my life. He was like a chiropractor,

Rolfer, acupressurist, you name it. After the session I said to God, "I did not know that it was possible to feel this good." I remember I had to sit on the ground and eat some peanuts to get grounded.

Going to the restaurant the man suggested was another, more intense story. The restaurant was down an alley, and it was very small. I walked in, and I was the only customer. The waiters bowed to me even more devotedly for some reason. I asked for number 14 on the menu. It was a soup with mushrooms floating on top. I remember it crossed my mind that these could be sacred mushrooms, but I quickly repressed that thought because it seemed ridiculous to have that in a restaurant. So I ate all the delicious soup. I barely made it home. (That week I was staying with a Balinese family because tourists had taken over my hotel.)

Soon I was in another dimension talking to Jesus, and I realized that in fact I had taken sacred mushrooms. I was shocked to look up and see this very handsome young Balinese man sitting on my bed. His teeth had been obviously filed in the tooth-filing ceremony I had heard about. They were so beautiful and straight. He seemed to be aware that I had taken the sacred mushrooms. He said, "What do you need? How can I serve you? Do you want me to make love to you?" I was so shocked I could not speak, and sometimes I regret not having taking him up on the latter.

The night Babaji called me to India was a real miracle.

He appeared to me in Bali wearing bright red and called me to India by waving his arms toward him and saying, "You come." I had no plans whatsoever to go to India at the time. I had no visa, no appropriate clothes for India, and certainly no tickets. But the next day there was actually a telegram from him in my screen door instructing me where to meet him in India! This I was in awe of, because I had told no one my address in Bali and he had obviously materialized the telegram! To get some of my papers in Bali, I had to get a cholera shot. The night I got cholera, the lights went out due to a storm and the flies attacked my body. I was delirious. I said, "I have become a carcass." By sunrise I was mysteriously healed, and I headed for Singapore to get my visa. I had resisted it, but it turned out to be one of the most important trips of my life. Still, it was hard to leave Bali.

PART TWO

RITUALS,
CEREMONIES,
AND FESTIVALS

WORSHIPPING THE DIVINE MOTHER

There is a 200,000-acre tract of land in Colorado called the Baca, where Hanna Strong has created a very unique spiritual community. This she did after nearly getting killed by a flying rock. She says she ran upstairs after that and dedicated her life to God. An Indian spiritual leader told her that the area was called the Bloodless Valley by the Indians because they considered it so holy that no wars were ever fought there. The Hopis had used it only for spiritual ceremony. When she went there, she was greeted by a man the locals called the Prophet. He knocked on her door and said, "So you have finally come." Then he proceeded to spell out a vision he had received that a woman like her would come and preserve all the world's faiths in this valley. The aim was to gather the world's major religions in one place in this awesome landscape.

There is a little defunct gold-mining town there named Crestone. It is kind of the end of the road in the middle of nowhere. The Strongs' Manaitou Foundation, financed chiefly by Laurance Rockefeller, gives the land away to any group that can articulate a serious spiritual mission. Those of us who are devotees of Babaji are fortunate to have received a piece of land where there has been built a very powerful Divine Mother temple. There is also a Zen Mountain Center, a mystical place for Carmelites, Buddhists, and others. The lamas love this area because it reminds them of Tibet. I love the area because it reminds me of the same feeling I experience in the Himalayan ashrams.

I remember so well many years ago when Muniraj and Shastriji came over from India to inaugurate the temple to the Divine Mother. The Hopis came also. They kept bowing to my gurus, and my gurus kept bowing to them. The respect that had for each other was overwhelmingly beautiful. Shastriji told us that where we had planted the murti of the Divine Mother was a very special spot. There was an underground lake beneath it which he could "see," and there was a crystal bed under that, he said. He also informed us that there was gold in the mountains but it should never be removed. What is so unique about this awesome valley in the mountains is that there is a mystical area of sand dunes, and there are also thermal hot springs.

I have seen so many healings take place at this spot. I have done God Trainings and initiations there often. On several occasions I received the information that this was a place of ascension. We call our ashram there the Haidakhandi Universal Ashram. Please call ahead of time (719-258-4108) to let them know you plan to visit. If you need healing, if you are distraught, if you feel your life or relationships are not working, or if you need spiritual uplifting, this is the place for you. Or you may just want to go worship. It is always best to stay a minimum of three days to get the best benefits.

NAVARATRI

Every year I also take people to the Himalayan foothills where we celebrate the *Navaratri* (the Divine Mother Festival). This is what I would call the final touch. You could also call it the tower of ecstasy, or maybe you could call it a real divine circus. (See my website for information.) If you cannot go to India with me, you can celebrate at any Babaji ashram around the world.

"Navaratri: Nine Days of Ceremony to the Divine Mother" By Marge De Vino, Ashram, Malmo, Nebraska

Recently Marge De Vino wrote about the Navaratri in her newsletter. (Here, it has been slightly edited):

Navaratri is a very special time of honoring the Divine Mother. Exact translation of the word *Navaratri* is "nine nights." Navaratri happens in the spring and in the fall of every year. It begins on the new moon. Each of the days honors a certain aspect of Divine Mother and gives a focus to the energy of that day. These are know as the *Nava Durga* (nine names of Durga):

Day One: **Sailapurtra**—Daughter of the Himalayas

Day Two: **Brahmacharini**—She who remains celibate

Day Three: **Chandraghanta**—She who is as beautiful as the moon

Day Four: **Kusmanda**—She who brings happiness

Day Five: **Skandamata**—Mother of Skanda, the leader of armies against evil

Day Six: **Katyayani**—Aspect of Mother Kali

Day Seven: **Kalaratri**—Kali night of no moon

Day Eight: **Mahaguri**—The great white goddess

Day Nine: **Siddhidatri**—She who is of great spiritual powers and knowledge

These days are also subdivided into three sets of three days:

Kali: The first three days are devoted to Kali, the goddess of destruction and restoration, wife of Shiva; it is a time of purification, a time to let go of all that is not "on purpose" for your life. This is like "cleaning out your closets" to make way for new things.

Lakshmi: The second three days are devoted to Lakshmi, the goddess of prosperity, wife of Vishnu; it is a time of preservation and taking care of things or acquiring what is necessary to make your life full of prosperity and fulfillment. This is like receiving the proper things you need to make your life happy.

Saraswati: The last three days are devoted to Saraswati, the goddess of wisdom, knowledge, and the arts, wife of Brahma; it is a time of receiving divine guidance on how to properly use all resources sent your way. This is like making more efficient and purposeful use of everything you are given.

All three aspects, in balance, are important for a fulfilling and happy life.

Traditional Ways to Honor Divine Mother during Navaratri

Usually, certain sacrifices or personal offerings are made during the nine days, such as giving up some certain food or drink or something you are accustomed to having or doing each day. Some people give up their favorite beverage, like coffee or tea; in the West, some give up watching TV or some other daily ritual they usually engage in.

You could also add something you don't usually do, such as reading the *Sapta Sati,* parts of the *Ramayana,* or other sacred scripture for twenty to thirty minutes each of the nine days. Whatever it is you choose, the idea is that each time you think of this thing you are doing, you offer up that thought and say a little prayer to the Divine Mother to increase your devotion to her. If you can continue your *sadhna* (spiritual practice) for the full nine days, there is a special reward from Divine Mother that happens on either the ninth or tenth day. She promises a personal physical experience of her. This is individualized, and only you will know what it is and when it has happened. It is up to you if you want to share it with anyone else after it happens. For some people, it makes it more real to share it; for some it is more powerful to keep silent about it.

The fifth day is considered the "turning point" day, when the cleaning/purification aspects are complete. The rest of the nine days get a little easier to handle on the day when the celebration is more than half completed. The energy of each day is building, so that by the end of Navaratri, there is much energy generated. Each fire ceremony becomes more and more filled with shakti (divine energy). For the highest benefits and greatest results of Navaratri, it is best to begin with the first day of Navaratri and continue to the end without missing any of the ceremonies. This requires some personal commitment and is definitely worth whatever it takes for you to be able to do it. Think of the great personal commitment and sacrifice performed by the Divine Mother in her care of each of us each day! It is awesome!

You are free to follow as many of these practices at home as possible to observe the nine days of the Divine Mother. You will, however, receive the greatest benefit by joining together with others at Haidakhandi temples—where the official ceremonies and observances take place.

"Worship to the Divine Mother"
(a speech by Shastriji)

The following is one of the many speeches Shastriji gave at Navaratris:

This whole world is made up of five elements, and there is nothing beyond it. So, with the same five elements, we can offer worship to the Divine Mother.

The first element is Mother Earth. (Yet according to the process of creation, the first element is ether and the last element is earth.) The definition of the element earth is smell, fragrance. That is why the first step in worshipping the Divine Mother is that we offer flowers full of fragrance, because with her grace, Mother Earth is producing beautiful fragrance, that is, flowers on earth. Now, a man might dedicate his whole life to create a flower, but even with total dedication, he cannot create a natural flower. When the Divine Mother has given us this gift through Mother Earth, it is our duty that we offer her own creation . . . the flowers. This is why we offer beautiful flowers to her as the first step in worship.

First of all, you fold your hands and meditate on the Divine Mother to call her. After that, you offer her a seat, and *asan*. And to give her a seat, you take a flower and put it there. This becomes her asan. Then you offer her water five times. First, to wash her feet. Second, you offer water with your hands. Third, you offer her water to drink. Fourth, you give her a bath, and fifth, you give her water to please her. Water too, is the Divine Mother's grace, because in spite of man trying, he cannot create even a single drop of drinking water.

We offer water these five times to show our gratitude, for it is her grace alone that she has given us this element of water, and without water we would all have died of thirst.

Then the third step is to show her the light element. This is why the Aarti is being done. Why would we offer her light? Because when the Divine Mother is seated before us and we are like an atom in comparison to her greatness, we offer her light as a symbol that it might remove the curtain of the darkness of ignorance separating us from her, so that this speck of light might unite us with her infinite light, so that we may become one with her.

After that, the fourth step is the element of wind. With it, we try to touch her, because the wind element is considered the element of touch. You will have seen that the pujari always waves a piece of cloth before the murti, after the Aarti—this is how it is symbolized that with each stroke we are touching every organ of the Divine Mother.

The last step is the bells and the mantras we sing, the Aarti we sing, because word and sound belong to the element of ether and with it we are in contact with ether. Apart from these five main elements, there is nothing on this earth which we can offer to the Divine. This is why we prostrate before her, telling her: This body is created by you, and I am offering my body back to you. This is the most basic principle of daily worship. By offering worship, one obtains complete mental satisfaction. To have mental satisfaction is the greatest gift to mankind.

Without Shakti, there is not *shaktiman* (that is, masculine energy). Without Shakti, nothing exists in the universe. It is indeed the duty of each of you to come to the Divine Mother Temple to offer worship to the Divine Mother. This is because the Divine Mother is the one who is protecting us from everything, and the one who is the one who gives us everything in the world. To the Divine Mother, you should offer your life and feel grateful that you are given the chance to live in this world. Because it is her grace.

Establish at different places temples of the Divine Mother. You will find peace only in the Mother.

Thank you, Shastriji, for this speech you gave in May 1985. If you want to help in being part of supporting Divine Mother temples please go to my website at www .sondraray.com.

THE FIRE CEREMONY

Sri Babaji renewed the fire ceremony to the Divine Mother that had prevailed in ancient times. The fire ceremony, or *yagna*, is based on scientific principles, and therefore is like the support of the earth. In the Vedas, it is written that the mouth of God is the fire. In the fire ceremony, one gives offerings to the Divine Mother along with mantras, and it reaches her in totality.

Shastriji explained to us that the law of nature, or life, is to give and take, as a farmer will sow a seed of rice in his field. He sows one seed but in return he gets much more than what he has sown. No computer can give you an account of how many billions of times a seed has given you more in return than what you sowed. That one grain of rice which you had sown will continue to give you tons and tons of rice, unless it goes bad.

It would be indeed very selfish of us, he said, that when the Divine Mother gives us so much food, so much grain to pacify our hunger and water to quench our thirst, we just keep on eating and drinking. But rather, it is absolutely justified that when the Mother gives so much, we should in return offer something back to the Mother and not just keep on eating it for our selfish pleasure.

A person who does not offer anything to the fire or to hungry people is concerned only with his own selfish hunger. Thus, he cannot reach the spiritual heights of the purity of the soul. To obtain happiness, bliss, and peace in life, one should always feed the fire and feed humans in need.

Babaji knew the fundamental way to give happiness to humankind, and this is how he started pleasing the Divine Mother, for the benefit of humankind, by doing fire ceremonies. Before Babaji appeared, there was famine in India.

After he appeared and started doing yagnas, India had a grain revolution.

"Sacred Fire"
by Mukunda

The following is a description of the fire ceremony, written by Mukunda:

This very ancient practice where people sit around the fire and make offerings and prayers (mantras and chants) is the fire ceremony. The fire is thought of by the yogis and seers as a representation of the Mother. The Mother is like the Sky. She remains always pure, untouched, uncontaminated, never stained by the phenomenal universe. . . . Just like the sky that remains sky no matter how many clouds appear. That undefiled nature of the Mother is you, it is me, it is essence of all form.

The offerings of fruit, flowers, rice, barley, etc. into the fire are symbolic of all the thoughts, all the words, and all the actions sacrificed into the fire of the Mother's love . . . the love that burns away all the clouds that cover our true nature. When the clouds are removed and the conditioned mind lets go, all fear, all doubt, pride, jealousy and envy are transcended and we enter the heart, the Mother. Then She speaks. She hears. She sees, and She moves all things. It is the Mother's love that liberates us from illusion. Alleluia.

THE CAVE

All of my childhood, I was "building" caves, mostly out of sticks along the railroad tracks. I was looking for a cave I could not find, so I built my own. Then I would sit inside, but I was never satisfied. In college, I took up spelunking and explored caves, but I did not like the bats too much. Later I explored lava caves in Hawaii with more gusto.

But I never felt satisfied until I found *the cave* that I had been looking for—the cave where Babaji first appeared in the foothills of the Himalayas and materialized his body in a ball of light, in 1970. In this the same cave, the great saint Mahedra Baba (Shastriji's first guru, who prepared the world for Babaji's return) first heard the Aarti. The Aarti is a service of prayers that are chanted. Literally, *Aarti* means "that which takes away pain." The Aarti service is highlighted by the waving of lights to the Mother and Sri Babaji. The flame symbolizes the removal of the darkness of ignorance. The Aarti is an ancient tradition, but it was told to me that some of the words of the modern version descended in gold to Mahendra while he was meditating in Babaji's cave. Some of the prayers are in Sanskrit and some are in Hindi.

I interviewed Gora Devi (a yogini from Italy) about the cave, because of all of Babaji's devotees, she had spent the most time with Babaji there. I figured surely he must have imparted great wisdom to her. Her answers were even more interesting than I had imagined they would be. Babaji had told her that the Mother *always* resides in the cave and that Babaji in his earlier form of Old Herakhan Baba had sat in that cave for twenty years! He dematerialized that body in 1922, and then, of course, he rematerialized another body in 1970 and stayed in the ashram for fourteen years. She also said there was an underground cave that had a secret passage to Benares. Well, I could believe that, because psychics I have taken into the cave had told me they could see that! Miracles are common in India.

Later Babaji installed the statue of Hairakhandeshwari above the cave. She is the "mother" of this place, and she is a combination of Kali, Lakshmi, and Saraswati. I have had amazing experiences taking my students into this cave. I take in about five at a time, and they can only stay in the cave for about fifteen minutes the first time. I have built up my nervous system over the years, so I can tolerate being in there all day with the students as they rotate. Several times in the beginning, however, I felt too much come up too fast.

My most interesting experience while being in the cave was the day I came out and heard that while we were in there, a huge miracle had occurred all over India. The murtis, or living statues, began "drinking" the milk that was offered to them by the people. As the people offered platters of milk to the murti, the milk would just disappear. People ran to get more milk and all over India stores ran out of milk. The BBC covered this amazing miracle, and we heard what was happening on a little radio someone had. Since Shastriji was right there at the ashram for Navaratri, I ran to him for a comment. He said, "Oh, Sondra, there is only a miracle like this every four thousand years!" Again, the Divine Mother was showing her power. If she can do that, think what she can do for us all.

THE HOPIS
Notes from a Lecture by Beth Hin

The Hopis have always said, and will continue to say, that you have to pay attention to Mother Nature and you have to be aware of the sacred space around you. They say that when you travel, you should ask for the "medicine" of each country to support you. And you should always embrace the native energy.

The Hopis say that we are entering the fifth world . . . the era of Truth and Illumination. In the fourth world, we got the lesson of "control," and it did not work. We were competing with God and not surrendering. But now they say, there is a new quickening of the planet and the descent of grace. However, this new era has people frightened, so you have to access the Great Tree of Peace. They say you should ask permission to manifest deepest truths.

The Hopis say we must unify the divine and the heart. They point out that we are constantly keeping away our connection with the highest mystical realms. They want us to remember that the depth of sacredness is life, and nature is so serious that we should never ever trivialize it.

The Hopis say that you have to live in a state of gratitude. You should not say: "I want_____, and when I get that, I will be grateful." You must say: "Thank you for what I have now." You must have satisfaction for whatever the Divine Mother is unfolding for you now! You should also say to others: "I am grateful you exist."

I remember very well being with the Hopi elders in the 1970s. We went to a site called Four Corners, where four states merge. It was the beginning of Rebirthing, and I was with Leonard Orr. Leonard started giving a talk about Rebirthing and how we use the breath. They listened to him patiently, but then they got up and gave their own speech. They said, "You think you know something about breathing? Every spring we get the plants to breathe and even the rocks to breathe!" So Leonard had to laugh at himself. Are they the real rebirthers or what?

Recently the Hopis elders came to our temple of the Divine Mother in Baca, Colorado. They had a pipe ceremony for International Peace Day. The Hopis have always embraced the Divine Mother. Embracing the Goddess always gives you a deeper love of creation.

THE VIRGIN MARY

Let's talk more about the Divine Mother in the form of the Virgin Mary. There are stories all over the world of miracles related to the Divine Mother in this form, but, here, I will focus on the Virgins of Venezuela. My very first trip to Venezuela was in the year 2000. I intuitively felt that, before I began my work, I should go to the sites where the Virgin had appeared. I soon began to see why the people of Venezuela had such open hearts.

We immediately went to visit the Virgen de Betania outside Caracas. The Virgin had appeared to a lady and told her that she wanted a sanctuary at that site. The lady went to the owner of the land and told him about the appearance. The owner immediately said, "Sure, I'll give it to you." I was told that when people go there, some get sparkles of red, violet, and green on their clothes. Someone found one in my hair, but sometimes people get them all over their body.

The next day we visited the Virgen de la Rosa Mystica. Her first appearance was in Montichiari, in northern Italy, in 1947. A nurse there had a vision of the Virgin floating in air, as a beautiful lady with swords. Later she appeared again in a hospital dressed differently. Instead of having swords, she had three roses: red, white, and yellow. The Virgen de la Rosa Mystica in statue form said she wanted to travel. She asked to be transported, and she came to Venezuela in recent years. She usually stayed one or two weeks in a home, and people would go to pray in that particular home.

The particular one I saw was in El Fuerte Tiuna (a military base). She appeared in a vision to an employee (a cleaner) and told him she wanted to go to a church in statue form, Convent Bethelem. He was afraid people would think he was crazy, so he did not want to take her. But the Virgin reappeared and said, "I told you, I want to go to the Convent Bethelem!" When I arrived, she had been there three years. After two weeks they wanted to move her, but they could not lift her at all. She would not budge. She got suddenly so heavy that not even three persons could lift her, which was amazing because she was small.

The main gatekeeper at the convent told me in Spanish that he had been crippled because of an accident. He was completely hunched over, and he could not lift his head. He asked the Virgin for a miracle. He began to walk the very next day! He also began to see the Virgin in tiny rocks. He gave me one and asked me to pray for Venezuela, almost as if he knew I was a teacher.

After my conference, I was lucky enough to be invited to the island of Margarita. A man in my seminar even paid for the hotel room for my co-worker and myself. I asked to go see the Virgin of the island—the Virgin of the Valley, she was called. Originally made in Spain, in 1530, she came to the island in 1911. The amazing thing is I was told that every home on the island has a Virgin Mary statue in their home. There are so many stories of miracles about her. One fisherman, for example, was looking for oysters when a sting ray hit him. This resulted in a huge wound that became infected and led to gangrene. The doctor told him that his leg would have to be cut off in order to save him. He told the Virgin of the Valley that if she would save him, he would offer her the first pearl he found. His leg was healed and he found a pearl that looked like a leg and had a scar exactly like he had! Unfortunately, the museum was closed the day I was there, but I was told there were arms made of gold from people who had been healed by her and that the whole place was full of miracles. Many couples have been reconciled, they said, and independence was won because they asked the Virgin for help.

SACRED RENEWAL BREATHWORK

For all of you who have ever dreamed of being reborn and starting life all over again, you can now make it possible. Breathwork (Rebirthing) merges the inner and outer breath, which creates a bridge between the physical and spiritual dimensions. This connection unites the human body to the prenatal life energy that built it originally and thereby rejuvenates the body and frees the individual consciousness from any kind of trauma, including birth trauma.

Rebirthing breathwork, which was founded by Leonard Orr, is a true spiritual gift. It has been my great joy to be a rebirther for nearly thirty years, and I am very grateful for the honor of being one of the first rebirthers on the planet.

In 2003, I was instructed by the Divine Mother herself to add Sacred Renewal Breathwork and to emphasize the Divine Mother energy by adding mantras and prayers to the Divine Mother during the Rebirthing session. My clairvoyant said that this made experiences nine times more powerful, while making the client feel safer at the same time.

Renewal breathwork is an experience of opening your breath so that a special flow of spiritual energy washes your mind and body with a divine bath. It is the science of letting in God's energy, wisdom, and love in order to experience the fullness of divine energy in the physical body.

This rhythmical circular breathing is done by pulling on the inhalation and relaxing on the exhalation in a continuous stream so that they are connected. This empties the negative mental mass out of your body and enables you to incorporate the life energy into your body instead. At some point, there is a reconnection to divine energy, and as a result you may experience tingling and vibrating in your body. This energy reconnects your body to the universal energy by vibrating out tension (which is the manifestation of negative mental mass).

This type of breathing in the upper chest can break you out of unconscious holding patterns in regard to breathing. The experience begins a transformation of the subconscious impression of birth from one of primal pain to one of pleasure.

We could say it is:

A baptism of the Holy Spirit with power

A physical experience of infinite being

A technique for spiritual healing

A rebuilding of the body with prenatal life energy

A removal of tension and blocks of full aliveness and health of the human flesh

A renewal of divine nature in human form

A regeneration of human perfection

A release of mortal bondage

A breathing mantra

A practical mystical experience

An inflow of divine energy

A growth experience focused on releasing the trauma rather than reexperiencing it

An energy release

A cure for subventilation

A learning to relax at the cosmic level

A cleansing of the mind and body of negative mental mass (tension)

A production of a perpetual state of health and bliss

A dynamic energy

A divine orgasm

A letting go to the natural pulsation that is in the core of the organism

A "youthing" process

An experience of God loving you at the cellular level

THE HEALING PROPERTIES OF REBIRTHING

We rebirthers tend to think of this process as the ultimate healing experience, because your breath, together with raising the quality of your thoughts, can heal anything.

Some of the physical conditions that we have seen Rebirthing eradicate are common colds, ulcerative colitis, backaches, poor eyesight, migraines, sinus trouble, throat and ear problems, respiratory illnesses, arthritis, epilepsy, dermatitis, and psoriasis. We have also seen emotional problems clear, such as claustrophobia, insomnia, sexual disorders, chronic distrust, fear of harm, anxiety, and depression. We are not therapists, and we do not treat these conditions. But with this work, a spiritual medium is provided whereby they can be understood, dealt with, and released.

I myself had had a pain in my body for twelve years (which started after my father's death), which dissipated in my first three sessions. I also began this work with hair loss and baldness, which started after my divorce. This took longer to heal, but the fact is, I got my hair back after breathing out the consciousness of loss. So you can imagine why I gave up nursing and became a rebirther!

The purpose of this work is not healing, but it has turned out to be a valuable by-product. The purpose is to acquaint people with a dimension of spiritual energy they may not have experienced until now. During this process, people are able to connect their illness or pain with the original negative thought behind it. We know that all pain symptoms stem from the effort involved in clinging to a negative thought. Some people are able to completely let go of the condition during the session. Others let go of it gradually during the weeks following the session by utilizing affirmations and the newly altered way of breathing. The breath is the cleanser of the body, just as the yogis always knew.

This work also improved my relationships greatly. One of the general benefits of the Rebirthing is the ability to receive love and have the direct experience of letting it in. During the session, you are physically able to feel the differences between resisting the love and letting it flow in (and touching is not required to get this experience).

The more they do this breathwork, the more people begin, as a result, to experience more and more bliss in their daily lives. People who continue the process also have more and more experiences of telepathy and intuitive knowledge, which again makes life more effective, fun, and interesting.

People report they have more physical energy and need less sleep. This is because the energy formerly used to keep the birth trauma suppressed is released and available for other, better things.

At the moment of birth, you formed impressions about the world that you have carried all your life, and these impressions control you from a subconscious level. Some of these negative preverbal thoughts are: Life is a struggle; The universe is a hostile place; The universe is against me; I can't get what I need; People hurt me; There must be something wrong with me; Life is painful; Love is dangerous; I am not wanted; I can't get enough love. Since negative thoughts produce negative results and since what you believe to be true, you create, just imagine how these birth thoughts are affecting your life!

The psychic and physical pain at birth is immense, and all this is suppressed. First, your umbilical cord was likely cut too fast—before you cleared your amniotic fluid from your lungs—and this caused a panic where you felt you would surely choke and die. Then, they likely turned you upside down and hit you to clear your lungs. This should never have happened. There is a lot of damage to the breath mechanism at that moment, and we don't breathe properly in life. One of the purposes of this work, then, is to heal the damage done to the breath mechanism at birth and to release those negative preverbal thoughts.

Release occurs when the client feels safe enough. This requires being in the presence of someone who has already released his or her own birth trauma. In the presence of a loving rebirther, trained in the wisdom of how spiritual energies work, a major healing of the birth trauma can take place. The negative thoughts you had about life and yourself while taking your first breath are the most damaging to your breath mechanism.

It is very important to continue so that you can have what we call a "breath release." This happens when you feel safe enough to relive the moment of your first breath. The breath mechanism then gets freed and transformed. From that moment on, a person knows when his breathing is inhibited and is able to correct it. The breath release is a critical release of all your resistance to life. This experience breaks that power of the birth trauma over your mind and body. The breath release comes easier for people who understand their unconscious death urge and have worked out a philosophy that includes the concept of physical immortality. (See chapter 9.)

You can achieve total recall of your birth scene, prenatal period, and even conception, believe it or not. Remembering the experience releases the pain and frees the mind and body. However, pieces of your birth can come up for years. We consider this breathwork a lifelong spiritual process. After you release your birth, you release past lives. There does not, however, seem to be any specific order to the memories. Sometimes people remember past lives sooner.

Life is very different after releasing the birth trauma. I cannot say enough about the benefits of this marvelous process. Most people tell us that this process delivered even more than they could have dreamed of. Even prosperity naturally improves, because people are able to let go of the thought "There is not enough." Rebirthing raises your self-esteem to a high level because you work out negative judgments you have about yourself you formed preverbally. And when you raise your self-esteem, all areas of your life are benefited.

The selection of a rebirther is a very personal task. In a sense, it can be thought of as choosing a compatible loving companion for a journey you will be taking. However, it is really *you* who has to do the breathing. There is a point where you will be able to do the process alone, but it is up to your rebirther to decide when you are ready. (It certainly would not be practical to try it on yourself until you have passed the infancy stage.) Leonard used to tell us that we should never give up doing Rebirthing until we could dematerialize and rematerialize at will. So this is an ascension process!

If you desire a rebirther approved by me, contact Tony Lo Mastro and Maureen Malone, Philadelphia Rebirthing Center (see page 241 for contact information).

PART THREE

THE JOY
OF LIFE

THE DIVINE MOTHER'S BOON OF
PHYSICAL IMMORTALITY AND ASCENSION

I have attempted to write about this subject since the beginning of Rebirthing in 1974. Thinking about it is one thing. Writing about it is another. And achieving it is way beyond all of that. My relationship to the subject keeps changing.

I started out wanting to live, period. Then I felt that it was mandatory for Rebirthers to master this knowledge. Then when I realized that there were, in fact, immortal masters mentioned in the Bible, I wanted to know how they became immortal. Before I knew it, I was obsessed with the whole subject, because I had so much death to process from my childhood. I could not stand the suffering of the people in my little hometown. I was required, like all the kids in my village, to attend every single funeral of anyone who died. I simply could not handle the statement of the church: "The

Lord took them away." It did not make any sense to me that God would kill people. So I rebelled, but I never stopped wondering why people died. The more I studied the subject of finding an alternative, the more interesting it got. Then I met other teachers who were teaching physical immortality. Finally, as I recounted in chapter 1, I actually met a four-hundred-year-old woman in India!

The first year of Rebirthing, I wrote a chapter in *Rebirthing in the New Age* on the subject of physical immortality. I was way ahead of my time, and I went through a crisis of aging while writing that chapter. I was only thirty-three years old. I found out that aging is controlled by consciousness, and I reversed all the symptoms by breathing them out. It took me nine years to get the courage to write a whole book on the subject. I called the book *How to Be Chic, Fabulous and Live Forever*. The problem, however, was the title. Bookstores put it under "humor" and not many readers found it. I regretted being so tongue-in-cheek with the title, because really it is a deep spiritual subject and the information in that book is very valuable.

A STEP TOWARD ASCENSION

Now my relationship with the subject is changing again. I feel that the knowledge of physical immortality is a vital step to the true initiation called ascension. I feel it is the supreme goal and can be achieved, as Jesus himself said. But it is a long path, and one has to surrender totally and has to be chosen for such initiations, as I understand it now. So it is something you have to work out with your Christ consciousness, the spiritual hierarchy, and the Divine Mother herself. The only purpose is for a mission of divine service. There can be no ego whatsoever involved in wanting to prove that you can live a long time.

In India, they say that only the Divine Mother grants the boon of physical immortality. I did not understand that when I started writing on the subject. I think I understand that better now. The Divine Mother is kundalini. It took me a lot of kundalini experiences to clear my past lives. It was often very difficult. I realize now why it is necessary to get past life memories out of the cells of the body in order to have longevity. It takes tremendous levels of consciousness and purity to withstand the might of kundalini. One has to go through the burning up of the old body and the building of the light body. (The light body is a body created from the light a person has manifested throughout all his incarnations).

Now I place the future in the hands of God. Physical immortality is still something I strive for, and it is a most awesome path. You have to understand how death works and how people die by squeezing out the life force with their own ego. Since we are here to clear our egos, we are all on the path of ascension whether we know it or not. We will have to get it in another lifetime if we don't get it in this one. So one might as well start now.

The Last Initiation

I found an article in India called "The Last Initiation," by Haridas Chaudhuri. It is the best summary I have found on the topic:

> Finally, the concept of immortality implies a harmonization of the entire personality and a transformation of the physical organism as an effective channel of expression of higher values. This may be called material immortality.
>
> There are some mystics and spiritual seekers who strengthen and purify their bodies just enough to be able to experience the thrilling touch of the Divine. They use the body as a ladder by climbing for which the pure spiritual level, the domain of immortality is to be reached. On attaining that level, the body is felt as a burden, as a prison house, as a string of chains that holds one in bondage. Dissociation from this last burden of the body is considered a *sine qua non* for total liberation.

Continued association with the body is believed to be the result of the residual trace of ignorance. When the residual trace of ignorance is gone, the spirit is set free from the shackles of the body.

The above view is based on a subtle misconception about the purpose of life and the significance of the body. The body is not only a ladder that leads to the realm of immortality, but also an excellent instrument for expressing the glory of immortality in life and society. It is capable of being thoroughly penetrated by the light of the Spirit. It is capable of being transformed into what has been called the "diamond body." As a result of such transformation, the body does not appear any more to be a burden upon the liberated self. It shines as Spirit made flesh! It functions as a very effective instrument for creative actions and realization of higher values in the world. It is purged of all inner tension and conflict. It is liberated from the anxiety of repressed wishes. It is also liberated from the dangerous grip of the death impulse born of self-repression. Mystics who look upon the body as a burden suffer from the anxiety of self-repression and the allurement of the death wish.

Material Immortality means decisive victory over both of these demons. It conquers the latent death instinct in man, and fortifies the Will to Live as long as necessary, as a channel of expression of the Divine. It also liquidates all forms of self-suppression and self torture and self mutilation. As a result, the total being of an individual becomes strong and steady, whole and healthy. There is a free flow of psychic energy. It is increasingly channeled into ways of meaningful expression. Under the guidance of the indwelling light of the Eternal, it produces increasing manifestations of Spirit in Matter.

I was given this page in India, and all I know is that the writer, Haridas Chaudhuri, wrote a book called *Being, Evolution and Immortality,* from which this essay was taken. Unfortunately, I have never seen the book, but I thank him for writing this essay, and I thank whoever handed it to me.

Why would anyone want to be physically immortal? Let's be clear once again that it is certainly not so that you can stay around and brag that you are two hundred years old. It is because you have accepted a mission of divine service and you want to remain healthy and strong so you can do that mission.

In the book *Aghora: At the Left Hand of God*, Robert Svoboda states the following: "Only those who go beyond time and space and causation to become immortal can be said to be truly in harmony with the cosmos and be truly healthy. Everyone who is doomed to live with a limited personality (ego) gets ill. Immortality is a desirable goal. It is infinitely more convenient to live through karmas all in one lifetime rather than to be forced to endure birth again and again and again" (p. 10).

The Divine Mother can cremate billions of karmas that fill the storehouse of the causal body, therefore freeing you from further obligation of being born in the world. She can alter all your patterns. She gives you the higher rebirth! Unless you clear the family imprint, you are not liberated. Liberation is our goal.

The Divine Mother can also plug you into the universal computer. I have seen how she has done that with my teachers in India. When you get to the point at which you are fearless, you get a "diploma," and after that you graduate. Then you might even be awarded clairaudience and clairvoyance. You get so you can go anywhere with your thoughts. Something else is directing your every move. Then it is absolutely marvelous to be alive, and you want to keep on living and serving.

As Leonard Orr said: "To master physical immortality, you have to master the philosophy of it, the psychology of it, and physiology of it." To grasp the philosophy of it, you need to be very clear that you are not separate from God and Spirit. You need to study the books on the philosophy of it.

To master the psychology of it, you need to unravel your death programming and unconscious death urge. To master the physiology of it, you need to understand that you are an energy system.

DEATH BY THOUGHT AND WORD

Since we are a product of our own thinking, the answer lies within. Jesus himself always said, "As a man thinks, so is he;" and "Thou art ensnared by the words of the mouth;" and "The power of life and death are in the tongue." He is clearly stating that what you say is what you get with your body. The body believes everything you say. So then if you want longevity, you have to stop saying "death is inevitable."

People age and die because they misuse the life force energy through the nature of their bad thinking. Divine substance is constantly available to everyone in equal amounts. (That is why the sacrament of physical immortality is available to all.) However, a person squeezes out the life force by indulging in limited negative thinking that crystallizes in the body and blocks the flow. There are spiritual masters that chose to consciously depart from the body, and that is a different story. They are taking samadhi rather than dying unconsciously.

A Course in Miracles says that death is a result of a thought called the ego, just as surely as life is a result of a thought called God. The ego is a false self we made up to compete with God. It is a collection of limited negative thought structures that prevent us from remembering that we are one with God. We unfortunately make these thoughts real and believe that that is who we are. We hang on to those negative thoughts by suppressing them in the body. This distorts the blueprint for new cells, causing the manufacturing of cells that are inferior to the ones being replaced. It is well known that the cells in the body are replaced every eleven months to three years. If healthy cells replace the old diseased unhealthy cells, then the aging process could be reversed. The blueprints are perfect when they leave their origin in spirit, because spirit is perfect. However, the vibratory frequency is disturbed by fear, guilt, anger, greed, insecurity, and other negative thoughts. Diseases are caused by strong, negative unbalanced thoughts that are embedded in the belief system and carried from life to life.

We have closed the door to self-knowledge and have allowed ourselves to be bombarded and brainwashed by outside programming. It takes courage and self-esteem to change programming. One has to be willing to investigate new concepts contrary to programming.

You can in fact demand in the name of I Am Presence

that your belief systems begin to get cleaned up. Sai Baba once said, "God equals man minus ego."

Gene Davis wrote a book called *Reversing the Aging Process*. He said: "The only way a thought or a thought pattern can be removed from the psychic field of the belief system is through etherealization by an energy with a higher vibratory frequency than that of the psychic field." That is why we need the help of a master. That is why we need Sacred Renewal Breathwork. That is why we need spinal analysis. That is why we need chanting, fire purification, and other spiritual purification techniques.

You could be reading all this and thinking that you do not qualify for such a high blessing as the way of everlasting life. However, as I mentioned earlier, the sacrament is being offered freely to all and this grace is equally available. *A Course in Miracles* says that miracles are ordinary, but purification is necessary first.

When we talk about this subject, we are not talking about being stuck in an old body. We are talking about getting a new body—the diamond body. This idea has nothing to do with feeling restricted to the body, either. For an immortal, the physical body is a liberated field. There is eventually complete mobility between planes.

Ann Lee Skarin gives the three divine laws for immortals in all her books: *love*, *praise*, and *gratitude*. The Bible says, "All things are possible." That statement means what it says. There are many immortals in the Bible. John 8:51 says, "I tell you this truth. Whoever holds fast to my teachings shall never enter the grave." Jesus is saying that it is possible for any of us to become immortal if we master certain spiritual laws.

Would you like to increase the quality of your life right now? Start freeing the energy of the past and the future, and put it all into the present! It is a here-and-now philosophy of life. It is not about running away from death. Immortals have died in many lifetimes and come back through reincarnation. They arrive at an incarnation where they are given a chance to do something different.

THE FRUIT OF YOUR LABOR

For immortals, their work is their joy. Work is worship, and immortals know this. The actual goal is to become an ascended master. *A Course in Miracles* speaks a lot about ascension. According to many teachers, this is now happening more on a planetary scale. There is a huge increase in the frequency of vibration. What is ascension, then? It is yet another leap into fifth-dimensional reality. Ultimately it means dematerializing into light and rematerializing. It is kind of like ice being heated to become water and then water being heated to become steam and then reversing the process. An ascended master can also rematerialize at will. In the Bible it is called translation. You surpass the birth-death cycle. You become ageless in the process.

Ascension means to embody the light and spirit of God. It is not an escape vehicle for unhappy beings who cannot resolve their world. It does not really even mean to depart. The being does not really go anywhere, so much as we cannot see them in the third-dimensional light.

This is an evolution that has to be earned. You can earn it by working through all your muck. We can actually now work through all our "stuff" without having to die. But you have to be ready to relinquish conflict in every form and make peace your number one priority. Are you ready to do that?

When you ascend, you fully inhabit the light body. The light body is a body created from the light that a person has manifested throughout all his incarnations. The consciousness would be of total joy, total unconditional love, and recognizing completely the oneness with the God head.

In order to ascend, you have to be complete on your *dharma* on the earthly plane. And then you will have the ability to dematerialize and rematerialize at will; and you can go anywhere needed or desired at will. One's ability to serve would really be enhanced. Jesus did this. Babaji does this. Many masters do this. There is also *bilocation* (being in two places at once) and *transfiguration* (changing into another person in order to do service work when you don't want anyone to recognize you). This I have seen Babaji do several times.

Eliljah (who is now about twenty-eight hundred years old) appeared to my friend Robert Coon and stayed floating in the air in front of him for four hours, while he transferred to him the knowledge of physical immortality telepathically. You can also read about another immortal master, the Comte de Saint-Germain, and how he appeared many places at once and helped our government. Beings who live in the fifth dimension are free to manifest multidimensionally. Every year I learn more about this. There definitely exists a priesthood of immortal ascended masters called the Melchizedek Priesthood. They are preparing the world for the return of the Holy Grail. Call on them. They will teach us if we open up.

The Bible says, "Ye who are grateful for all things, your body shall be filled with light and ye shall comprehend all things." Since the ascension attitudes are love, praise, and gratitude, I would like to end this chapter with a gratitude prayer I wrote many years ago when I was in a supreme state of appreciation for my life and career. I hope it inspires you. Although my life has been, at times, extremely hard and sometimes I failed to feel thankful, I was very sincere when I wrote this, and I do know that gratitude is the answer.

Prayer to the Divine Mother

Thank you for the original spark of life I was given . . . the chance to live, the opportunity to be. Thank you for creating me in your image. Teach me how to live up to that. Thank you for all my past lives of learning which have prepared me for this moment. Thank you for the correct choice of parents, the ancestors who fit so well into the scheme of things. I am forever grateful for the moment of my conception, for the joy of it and for being wanted.

Thank you for the protection I had in the womb, the glory of developing a body there, and for the miracle of this possibility. Thank you for my birth at home in this life . . . for all those present who were there for me, for the freedom my mother had to move about, and for the spirit of things on that day in August.

Thank you again for the parents you chose for me, which were perfect for me this time around. My mother, for her wisdom, positive attitude (and lack of complaining); for her honesty, hard work, and holiness. My father, for his love and fun and brilliance and creativity; and even for his severe illness which tempered me like fire shapes steel. For my sister, who challenged me all the time . . . who in the end made me humble. Thank you for my town where I grew up . . . the sweetness and the kindness of all three hundred of them. All the love they gave me constantly. The holiness of the farmers, the integrity they demonstrated to me, the honesty and deep truth they taught me. Thank you for the experience of being "known," exposed completely; and the intimacy of that, which prepared me for fame. Thank you for the necessity it all gave me for having to be accountable at all times.

Thank you for the religious teaching I had, and especially the relationship to Jesus and the very foundation of that spirituality in the core of my being. Thank you for all the teachers of my youth, especially my sophisticated fifth-grade teacher and, more than anyone, my typing teacher.

Thank you for the teamwork I learned playing basketball, the experience of winning and being on a winning team.

Thank you for my college education and especially for the guidance toward my choice of career as a nurse.

Thank you for the difficult marriage I had, which taught me that I needed to study relationships.

Thank you even for the mistakes and extreme difficulties I have had. They have shaped my character and life and taught me all too well how things really should be. They spurred me on with great drive to study and accomplish many important things.

Thank you for giving me the absolute privilege to be a pioneer in the Peace Corps and Rebirthing.

Thank you with all my heart for leading me to the saints and gurus who have taken me under their wing and have given me frequent experiences of divine intoxication. Oh, please make me like them.

Thank you for life itself and all its wonders. For the energy you have given me. Thank you for the life that is still around, the Infinite Spirit in all things, the vitality of being, the opportunity, the chance to partake and use this spark of life.

Thank you for my body and its perfection, for the fact that I am a woman. Thank you for the ability I have been given to move, to speak, to feel, to touch, to see, to hear, and especially to write.

Thank you for my health and especially for the body's ability to heal itself of all the conditions that I have mistakenly created. Thank you for my mind and the ability to think to correct myself. Thank you mainly for the many times my life has been saved.

Thank you for continually teaching me the highest truths, for choosing me to lead the people to more enlightenment, for my chance to serve you in every way possible. Thank you for all the adventures of my life and all the wonderful people you place before me . . . for the gifts of all my friends and colleagues. Thank you for helping me every time I needed it and for answered prayers.

Oh, please liberate me from all bondage.

And as my guru Shastriji wrote it, ever so much more beautifully:

Oh my mind, always remember her who is the giver of life and who appears like the full moon from a sea of bliss and consciousness; radiant with divine brilliance, she graces her worshippers by appearing before them. From her flows the nectar of beautitude. It is she who dissolves the sins of the world, like the purifying waters of the Ganges. Meditate on the Mother as the only one who can give you true blessing.

SERVING HUMANITY

My master Babaji always said that the formula for happiness is love, truth, simplicity, and service to humanity. He also mentioned the importance of chanting the mantra "Om Namaha Shivai" for purification. The spiritual masters look not at a person's status but rather at a person's motives that prompt his activities in the world, and they also look at the effect of his influence upon others. True service is a spontaneous outflow of a loving heart.

I was lucky that I grew up in a small village in Iowa (population three hundred). Perhaps because of that, service came naturally to me. Or maybe it was because of my training in past lives; or probably it was because I have been a devotee of Babaji in many lives. Anyway, I would go around town on my tricycle (I started early), and later on my bike, to visit the sick and the poor and the elderly who lived alone. I always knew how to cheer them up. Kids are natural healers if you let them go for it. There was no one stopping me. I had the advantage of being in a setting where my mother never had to worry about me when I was out and about. It was a close-knit community. Everyone knew everyone else, and so everyone had the right to parent me.

I always thought I was supposed to be a missionary. I was a waitress first to make money for college. Then I became a nurse. Then I became a rebirther. Then I became a writer. Then I became a public speaker. All service careers. But joining the Peace Corps soon after nursing school was my real boot camp for world service! That, above all, got me in shape for serving humanity in a way that could potentially make a real difference.

All this was long before I ever found the book *Serving Humanity,* by Alice Bailey. That book leaped off the shelf at me, almost literally, at a friend's home. The book blew me away, and I was very grateful that somehow I had been on the right track even before I found it. That book straightened me out even more, though, and I dare you to read it. It will straighten anyone out.

Babaji used to yell at us, "Work is worship and idleness is death!" Work dedicated to God is called karma yoga. The best work is serving humanity at a very high level.

THE JOY OF A LIFE OF SERVICE

You may already be in a service-oriented career. If you are not, you might consider these two choices: change careers *or*, if you do not want to change careers, figure out how to make your work more service oriented. All work could be considered service, if you have the right attitude. But if you cannot seem to muster that positive approach in your current situation, then something should change. Your line of service could be cultural, political, scientific, religious, philosophical, psychological, financial, or whatever. If you are unclear what it should be, start by offering up your willingness for the divine plan of your life of service to manifest.

Are you willing to be part of the new group of world servers? Alice Bailey asked that. It is our task to aid the work of the spiritual hierarchy, as it is responsible for the evolution of the planet. The masters are always searching for those who are sensitive to the plan, those who have no selfish motives, those who desire nothing but to serve. The masters are busy preparing those souls for constructive work and eventually for initiation. Her very profound book explains how the system works and how souls earn the right for higher initiation based on levels of service.

Imagine the person who is deluded by the idea that there is no other way but his way, or the person who is oriented by the expression of his personality. Imagine the person who is run by sheer ambition, addiction to competition, the glamour of personal ego power, and the accumulation of material things. Imagine the person who is responding merely to physical needs and the satisfaction of desires, or the person who is jealous of others. Imagine the person who is largely self-centered. Finally, imagine the risk this kind of person runs of making huge mistakes and accruing karma.

Now imagine a person who has achieved peace and quiescence, whose very brain cells are falling into the larger divine rhythm. Imagine a person who has love for all beings, irrespective of who they may be, the person who is determined to do what is best for all of humanity. Imagine the person who has right thinking, decent behavior, and constant kindness. Imagine the person who works on achieving constant inner spiritual growth, whose character is essentially humility, who is constantly working to purify himself and then making a difference for humanity.

Now then, which deserves to live in the aura of the masters and receive the higher initiations? The answer is so obvious that it is nearly trite to write this. However, some people may not even realize which category they are in because they are so busy that they have never even thought about all this.

Regarding yourself, always remember: Be ready to change your point of view when a higher, better way is presented to you. Avoid hanging on to the past and staying stuck in ancient ideas and imposed authorities. Remember you are connected to divine intelligence. Evolve! Advance!

Ask yourself whether you are of any use to the masters or a burden to this planet. It is not too late to change. If you are a burden, you don't have to commit suicide. Babaji always said, "There is no saint without a past, and no sinner without a future." Start now to cultivate a higher sensitivity.

Serving Humanity points out that as your love for humanity increases and your interest in yourself decreases, so you will move toward the center of light and love, where the masters stand. And if you are of the proper caliber, you might be chosen for initiations. When a master turns in your name as a candidate for initiation, you enter a preparatory process so that revelation can be brought to you. Revelation and evolution go together. If you think about it, this makes total sense. The greatest respect is due Alice Bailey and the Tibetan master Djwhal Khul for this book, which explains so beautifully how things work and what is going on and should be going on. As the book says, "Sooner or later a soul arrives at the realization of the futility of material ambition. This could take eons of lifetimes. But when the soul arrives at this point, a high state of integration is marked and there is a huge shift of consciousness. The soul then longs to function as part of the greater Whole."

The authors also relay that if you are not yet at that point, you should "stand on the side of those who are silently and steadily building a new order." Lend your support, they say: "If you cannot yourself, teach or preach or write, give of your thoughts and of your money so that others can."

Beings of financial stature who regard money as a responsibility to be dispensed wisely in the service of others should be honored for their understanding of the right use of money. There is, in fact, a whole chapter in *Serving Humanity* called "Money in Service." Naturally, they say, "Billions which go the way of armed conflict in all nations must be deflected towards those expenditures which will make the plans of the Hierarchy possible." On page 379, there is this beautiful prayer:

> Oh Thou in Whom we live and move and have our being, touch the hearts of men everywhere so that they may give to the work of the Hierarchy that which has hitherto been given to material satisfaction. The New Group of World Servers needs money in large quantities. I ask that vast sums be made available. May this potent energy of Thine be in the hands of the forces of light.

Let us all learn the right expression of our divinity together. Let us make this book required reading on all college campuses.

DIVINE MOTHER FESTIVAL IN INDIA

In India, they say there is nothing higher than the worship of the Divine Mother. Every spring and fall people gather for the purpose at Navaratri and worship the Divine Mother for nine straight days starting at 5 AM and running to 9 PM. The celebration is always conducted according to perfect Vedic astrology, and Babaji once told me that it would take twelve years to make the spiritual progress on the outside that you can make in just one day at Navaratri. So that is why I go no matter what and why I always truly acknowledge those who come with me.

I would never complain about the so-called inconveniences of India. I'd rather spend ten days giving up American conveniences than battle out the ego for lifetimes. Besides, my experience is that people get so high in this festival that the inconveniences become next to nothing. In 2004, at the Divine Mother Festival in Herakhan, my group said that the room where they had to all live together with their sleeping bags looked like a challenge at first. As the days went on, it began to appear to them like a palace. This year I had mostly Australians, one Spaniard, one Frenchman, and one New Zealander. It was the easiest group on record for me. Nobody got sick and nobody had any accidents. They all took care of each other because they had all been rebirthed and knew how to process themselves.

Upon arrival in Delhi, we heard that Amma was in town. I was thrilled. Any chance to see the Divine Mother in the flesh is a miracle and worth the crowds. Rama Pilot, a female politician, came to meet me and we went together. We were lucky to get a hug from Amma, and I felt this was a good omen for my group. The last minute before leaving for the ashram, her daughter asked me what it would take for me to start seminars in India. I blurted out, "Thirty women." She said, "I can produce forty." Wow! For years I had been waiting for the right organizer and the right moment to start, and here it was.

The next morning I got on the bus with my group for the long ten-hour ride to Haldwani. Everything was fairly smooth except that, after about seven hours, the bus broke down. I went around and processed each person on their fear or resistance to going to Herakhan, and just when I finished the process, the bus got going. In Haldwani that night, I rebirthed everyone, and the next morning we jumped in the jeeps. I told everyone to stay in silence during the trip and to observe their mind. What transpires right before you first enter to Herakhan is always amazing. One girl related the following about that trip: "I have been married umpteen times and fallen in love so many times; but never ever have I felt love like I felt approaching Babaji's ashram."

The ashram was pretty full, so my students had to stay in one big room together, which meant they would have to undress in front of each other. (Usually men had one dorm and women another.) I asked them to try not to complain, but I thought it would push all their buttons. In fact, they handled it really well. In the end, they even liked it, because they constantly supported each other when they were trying to process their experiences.

I went to Babaji's cave with my organizers, Peter and Pauline, to charge up. We stayed about a half hour, and being there for that length of time is so powerful that you always have some reaction. My teeth started feeling strange. How often do you start feeling your teeth?

At the chai shop, a gal approached me who had come alone. She informed me that over the past year she had had repeated dreams of me and the Comte de Saint-Germain. She told me Saint-Germain would appear and be very concerned about me. I told her that made sense, because I had

had to go through the dark night of the soul, and it had been really hard. It was nice to hear that the immortal masters were helping me. In Herakhan, everything anyone says to you is an important message. The place is such a sea of consciousness that the very person you are supposed to meet always shows up at the right time and you have the exact experience you are supposed to have. This phenomenon increases daily as the energy rises.

A PACKED SCHEDULE

The first day the group had a bit of a hard time adjusting to all the ceremonies and the schedule. Some went into resistance about the intense schedule. But, I told them, the more you go along with the intense schedule, the sooner your case is cracked.

The first night an old yogi named Prem Baba took samadhi (a conscious departure from the body). I had known him fairly well since my first visit in 1977. I was especially struck when the younger yogis told me in the morning that they had carried his dead body to a taxi and sat him up in the lotus position in the back seat! They all commented how beautiful he looked as he was sent off to his village. The image remains in my mind.

The second day we started the head shaving down by the river. I never insisted my group do this process, called *mundun*, but after I explained the immense value of it, several were eager to do it. So I had each person choose a support buddy who would gather the equipment, find the barber, and get the banana leaf on which the hair would fall so they could float it down the river. We always held a ceremony in my group for mundun. The person who was about to do it would kneel down in front of the barber (who looks the same as he did in 1979, when I first did mine); the buddy would be there for support, and the rest of the group would chant "Om Namaha Shivai."

On the third day I was invited to sit around the fire with the male yogis and make an offering during the fire ceremony. This I did as a leader in a way that represented all the women there. It was extremely crowded in the circle, and I was hemmed in between the men. I did not mind this, as I am very used to India and I was just so grateful to be invited. I began offering the fruits, flowers, grains, and incense every time we said "Swaha." Then, suddenly my bliss was over and my knees began hurting more than you can imagine. The pain was so intense I thought I would pass out. I knew this pain was not just because I was sitting in the lotus position, nor was it because I was jammed in with the others. I had been in those positions many times. I continued the ceremony, and at the end I could hardly get up. But then so much happened I forgot all about it . . . for awhile.

In the afternoon I asked two yogis to speak to my group, Bo from Sweden and Harigovind from Switzerland. My group was mesmerized by them and their stories of Babaji and life at the ashram. I forgot all about my knees. But that night they hurt a lot, and so I asked an acupuncturist to my room. He is one of the best in the world, but when I told him my problem he remarked, "I know so many women your age with this condition." I blurted out, "I refuse to buy into that! I don't accept ideas of old age." He said, "Yes, but I know the body." This upset me more. I knew it was just my mind. My roommate and assistant, Shanti, was really disturbed by his comment, and she got out her divining rods and started asking me questions. Yes, of course, the fire at the ceremony had brought up a past life in me. We got that far before we were interrupted by important matters with the group.

On day four I had a phenomenal dream. I was in an audience looking at a stage. Suddenly these immortals started walking by in very unusual outfits. I was told they were each hundreds of years old. They looked as though they were thirty or forty, and they walked across the stage in such a limber fashion—almost like they were dancing—that I was filled with delight. I wanted to talk to them, and I felt absolutely elated that I was at least given a glimpse of them.

When I awoke, I was certain that it was not just a dream, and I was told that the immortals visited me, which I believed. What a blessing!

On day five I took my whole group to see the guru Muniraj to receive their names. This was a very, very special moment for them, and I told them to bathe and to dress in their finest garb. Receiving a name from the guru is special, because Muniraj goes into a certain state of consciousness and reviews one's whole past and one's whole future quickly and then channels a name that pulls the two together. It is simply astounding how perfect the meaning of the names comes out. On some occasions, the name does not come right away, so Muniraj simply picks up the newspaper and reads it, waiting for the name to come, which of course drives the student up the wall. On this day we were crammed in his room, because I had agreed to join the Swedish group to make it easier on Muniraj and cut down the number of days he had to spend on this. He was in great form! The names all came with lightning speed, and he stunned us with the perfection of each one.

After this I took the group into Babaji's private receiving room to meditate. This is where he received dignitaries. The unique thing about it is that there is a big mirror on one wall and a swing facing it. Babaji loved swings. I heard that he used to take dignitaries there and make them sit in the swing and look at themselves in the mirror. What a great process! On occasion when I go into the room, the swing has started moving on its own, as if he were there.

That night, when Shanti and I lay in our beds for our evening meditations, I saw a crystal in my third eye. Now, I am not a very visual type—really I'm more auditory— so when I see something like that, it is a real treat. I was told this was the crystal of knowledge and things would be downloaded as needed. Needless to say, I was in immense gratitude.

On day six, the yogi Rai Dass, from Germany, spoke to us by the cave. He is such a delight, and his words dance on your mind as if you could see them bouncing along. He always impresses me so much, because he speaks seven languages fluently, which is nothing compared to his supreme devotion to Muniraj. The group was in rapture once again, and I was glad that I had spent so many years developing my relationships with these yogis who give so much to my groups.

This was the day I told the group they had to take everything out of their dorm room, air out their sleeping bags, clean it up immaculately, and change all the locations of where they slept. This went off with no hassle. After that we all lay down and breathed.

GROUP SURRENDER

By this time eleven out of the seventeen in my group had shaved their heads without my prompting. This was a lot of surrender. We did not make wrong in any way those who chose not to. They all said they would do it in another year when they felt more ready.

There was only one gal in the group who was not letting go. I expected her to crack in the cave, but even that did not work. Her birth had been all the "last minute," so I told her I was sure she was not going to let go until the last minute and I was not worried. On day nine she shared her frustration with the group. She was really stuck. I suggested she lie down on her sleeping bag on the terrace and let the whole group rebirth her. They all sat around her with love and compassion. I started things off, and then I stepped back and let the group take the lead. This turned out to be a phenomenal experience for all, and she finally let go.

Shanti told me she was down by the cave and a yogi told her to go in and do a certain mantra. She did that, and lo and behold, there was another yogi there explaining puja; so she invited him to our group. I was delighted, because the yogi I had asked to speak on that day could not make it. So here we were with this new yogi, named Freedom. He explained to my group all the intricate meanings of the pujas and ceremonies, and he took us all deeper than we ever imagined. I had never even met this yogi before. What victory for us all!

Day nine is the final fire ceremony at Navaratri, and the energy is higher than you can imagine. After it is over, and the ashes cool, we are allowed to take home a small container of the ash, which is very holy and powerful. It contains all the offerings and mantras and love from the whole nine days. This proved to be my saving grace later on. Right after the final fire ceremony, I took my assistant Shanti and my organizers Peter and Pauline into the cave to offer our thanks. I kept thanking Babaji for the wonderful, wonderful experience we all had, for the wonderful group I had had, and for all the blessings and spiritual alchemy we all experienced. In my head I heard him say, "It is all by the grace of the Divine Mother."

I was finally able to let Shanti rebirth me that night. Still having trouble with my knees, we started processing the past lives involved. On the tenth day, when the weddings are performed, I at last had some relief. A beautiful sacred dancer performed for the brides and grooms (several couples getting married around the fire). She was excellent, except her sari kept falling off. Oh well. Shanti and I asked Freedom to give us a Vedic astrology reading. What a way to end the festival!

ANOTHER LESSON

The next day we were all ready to go at 6 AM. We waited and waited and waited. This turned out to be a big *lila* (a divine lesson of the master) for my group. After all, they had had it easy. There had been no major incidents for this group, which was unusual. Nobody got sick or had an accident. I was bragging about my group, and you know what happens when you brag. There was a huge mix-up and no jeeps had even been ordered . . . and there we were. We could not even leave the ashram. So the waiting process began. We had to reorder the jeeps and then wait the many hours before they arrived.

It is always an interesting spiritual test when there is a crisis. You find out if you are high enough to handle it without any upset. I learned a lot about people that day. When the jeeps finally came, I told everyone to be in silence on the way back to Haldwani so they could integrate the experience. Once there, we had to face the ten-hour bus tide back to Delhi. Everyone was in a huge process. It was truly interesting. I was in my own process because my knees started really hurting again. I thought I was through those past lives, but apparently I was not. So I told Shanti, "Well, I am just going to rub sacred ash on them every hour and see what happens." And that is what I did on the bus ride.

Upon arriving at the hotel in Delhi at 10 PM, I had a major kundalini experience, and the stuck energy in my knees moved up. Some of it went out and some it stuck in my head. But at least I could say I did not have arthritis, rheumatism, or any other condition from aging. I was thrilled but kind of spaced out. Somehow I misplaced things, and when I got to Singapore I discovered all my earrings were gone. Another lila. Oh well, so what? We'd had the time of our lives. My group laughed at me in the Singapore airport and started processing me on how I created that.

When I got back to L.A., my roommates simply could not believe that I was getting on another plane in two days and going to Washington, D.C., to a Mary Magdalene Conclave. How could I *not* be there? It was deliberately planted right next to the Pentagon. We did two and a half days of prayers to all the Divine Mothers of eleven traditions, with Tom Kenyon taking the lead. My eyes were watering the whole time, as I still had not integrated my experiences in India, but then there was a miracle at the last minute. I manifested a woman with divining rods, who took me further through the past lives that had been activated by the fire.

I would not have missed that conclave for the world. Could we change the world? No, but we could make the world a more benevolent place, which we did. Right after that, one of my friends there married a 9/11 widow. It was amazing.

Next, I was off to work in St. Louis. I did a women's group to initiate them into the Divine Mother, as Babaji had requested. They loved it. Then I spoke in the Church of Religious Science and also at both church services, after which we had a group Rebirthing right in the sanctuary. Now that was a dream of mine for sure.

Om Para Shaktieye Namaha! (I bow down and give salutations to the supreme energy of the universe, the Divine Mother!)

MEDITATIONS AND PRAYERS

The following was given to me by my guru Shastriji, to whom I have dedicated this book.

Sit before your altar with a picture of the Divine Mother on the altar: (Mother Mary, Amma, Quan Yin, Lakshmi, or whomever you relate to. You can order a photo of Amma from her website www.Amma.org.)

> Prepare offerings of flower petals on a beautiful cloth before you. Sit in the lotus position in front of the altar with the flower petals between you and the altar. Your hands should be washed. The candle on your altar should be lit and your favorite incense offered to the Mother. Wave the newly lit incense in front of the Mother's picture and then bow. Begin the ceremony by repeating out loud "Om, I bow to her, the mother of the

universe . . . Swaha" [and continue with all 108 names as listed on pages 173–79]. When you say *Swaha*, toss a petal to the Mother on the altar in front of the Mother's picture. [*Swaha* means "I offer myself." It is like putting a stamp on the letter. You don't send a letter without the stamp. Swaha makes sure it gets to the Mother.]

Before each line repeat, "Om, I bow to her . . . " If you do this with others, you must all be saying everything in unison, and each person should have a copy to read from.

Shastriji said we should try to embody these qualities of the Mother in ourselves. So pay attention to what you are reading, and take it into your heart.

The first time I ever did this prayer, there was a miracle. I landed in Stockholm, Sweden, from India. I sat before my altar in my hotel room and repeated the 108 names of the Divine Mother. Immediately after finishing, the Divine Mother gave me an amazing gift: A new training came into my head totally complete. It was an advanced wet Rebirthing training. I jumped in my bathtub with my snorkel and tried to do it, but it was very challenging. It took me a while to learn the techniques. I called it the Liberation Training after I learned it. When I tried it on Don McFarland, the founder of Body Harmony, he came flying up out of the water and said "*This* is a stroke of genius." I said, "It is not from me, it is straight from the Divine Mother." He liked it so much we decided to try the training together in Iceland, so we could be out in the thermal pools for the instruction. That training was so powerful that it took me nine months to integrate it myself.

I have often done these prayers with my students in a group. I tell them to ask the Divine Mother for one thing they want before we start. One female in Venezuela asked the Mother to be healed of her infertility. A year later when I landed in Caracas, there she was at the airport with a newborn baby girl she had named Sondrita Luz. There are many stories like that. The Mother is very generous.

The 108 Names of the Divine Mother

Om, I bow to her,

1. The mother of the universe . . . Swaha

2. Who resides in the heart of the master . . . Swaha

3. Who gives birth to the worlds . . . Swaha

4. Who is full of boundless mercy . . . Swaha

5. Whose form is blissful . . . Swaha

6. Who is worshipped by the worlds . . . Swaha

7. Who is the supreme goddess . . . Swaha

8. Who is the Mother as a warrioress . . . Swaha

9. Who bestows good fortune . . . Swaha

10. Who is divinely beautiful . . . Swaha

11. Who is the embodiment of knowledge . . . Swaha

12. Who is prosperity . . . Swaha

13. Who sustains all the world . . . Swaha

14. Who is the goddess of heaven . . . Swaha

15. Who reads all minds . . . Swaha

16. Who gives victory to her devotees . . . Swaha

17. Who is divine energy . . . Swaha

18. Who is worshipped by divinities . . . Swaha

19. Who looks after the universe . . . Swaha

20. Who removes all fear . . . Swaha

21. Who gives divine protection . . . Swaha

22. Who is the goddess of the waters . . . Swaha

23. Who fulfills all desires . . . Swaha

24. Who is the mother of the three worlds . . . Swaha

25. Who gives liberation . . . Swaha

26. Who is the goddess of fortunes . . . Swaha

27. Who resides in the lotus . . . Swaha

28. Who is worshipped by God . . . Swaha

29. Who is full of power . . . Swaha

30. Who removes the troubles of the universe . . . Swaha

31. Who gives birth to all . . . Swaha

32. Who is the consort of victory . . . Swaha

33. Who is the royal majesty . . . Swaha

34. Who is the goddess of gods . . . Swaha

35. Who resides in the heart of the king of sages . . . Swaha

36. Who showers the nectar of grace . . . Swaha

37. Who is the power of consciousness . . . Swaha

38. Who is the maker of destiny . . . Swaha

39. Who is beyond all things . . . Swaha

40. Who is full of mercy . . . Swaha

41. Who is the goddess of the planet . . . Swaha

42. Who is the goddess of perfection . . . Swaha

43. Who is the power of the beginning . . . Swaha

44. Who resides in Jerusalem . . . Swaha

45. Who is inaudible sound . . . Swaha

46. Who is supreme might . . . Swaha

47. Who is energy everlasting . . . Swaha

48. Who is knowledge of the beyond . . . Swaha

49. Who is glorified by the scriptures . . . Swaha

50. Who is indestructible . . . Swaha

51. Who is the great fighter . . . Swaha

52. Who is transparent like a crystal . . . Swaha

53. Who breathes as the children . . . Swaha

54. Who breathes as the children . . . Swaha

55. Who breathes as the children . . . Swaha

56. Who showers the nectar of love . . . Swaha

57. Whose every organ is the source of light . . . Swaha

58. Whose nature is joyful . . . Swaha

59. Whose voice is most sweet . . . Swaha

60. Who is praised by perfected souls . . . Swaha

61. Who is the power of the origin . . . Swaha

62. Who removes all pain . . . Swaha

63. Who crushes pride as the enemy . . . Swaha

64. Who heals all wounds . . . Swaha

65. Whose light shines as the full moon . . . Swaha

66. Who accepts all surrender . . . Swaha

67. Who is sacrifice . . . Swaha

68. Who is the principle power . . . Swaha

69. Who is the power of Om . . . Swaha

70. Who is divine sound and light . . . Swaha

71. Whose body is the universe . . . Swaha

72. Who resides in the heart of Hairakhandi Shiva . . . Swaha

73. Who is Tara, destroyer of the dark forces . . . Swaha

74. Who is the goddess of the goddesses . . . Swaha

75. Who gave birth to the savior . . . Swaha

76. Who is the embodiment of mercy . . . Swaha

77. Who is without blemish . . . Swaha

78. Who protects the three worlds . . . Swaha

79. Who gives shelter to all . . . Swaha

80. Who is the embodiment of divinity . . . Swaha

81. Who is the enchantress of all . . . Swaha

82. Who is the mother of fire . . . Swaha

83. Who removes poverty and misery . . . Swaha

84. Who gives nutriment in plenty . . . Swaha

85. Who is the breath of the wind . . . Swaha

86. Who is the object of meditation . . . Swaha

87. Who annihilates all fear . . . Swaha

88. Who is praised by both Gods and demons . . . Swaha

89. Who is the queen of the battlefield . . . Swaha

90. Who holds the rosary, conch, and flower . . . Swaha

91. Who shines like the stars . . . Swaha

92. Whose glory is sung by Brahma, Vishnu, and Shiva . . . Swaha

93. Who is the embodiment of all riches . . . Swaha

94. Who is ever ready to protect all people . . . Swaha

95. Who is the celibate goddess . . . Swaha

96. Who is the protectress of the gods . . . Swaha

97. Who is the giver of all strength . . . Swaha

98. Who is the giver of ecstasy . . . Swaha

99. Who is awe inspiring . . . Swaha

100. Who is pure nectar . . . Swaha

101. Who is the source of desire . . . Swaha

102. Who wears the crown of glory . . . Swaha

103. Who is the ideal of nations . . . Swaha

104. Who is first amongst the brave . . . Swaha

105. Who drinks the nectar of the lotus . . . Swaha

106. Who blesses the whole world . . . Swaha

107. Who sends the light force . . . Swaha

108. Who graces the whole universe . . . Swaha

PRAYERS WRITTEN BY SHASTRIJI

The following excerpts are from *Haidiyakhandi SaptaSari* (Seven Hundred Verses in Praise of the Divine Mother of Haidakhan), by Shastriji. This book can be ordered from the Babaji Ashram:

O Universal Mother, you give me shelter. In truth, you are the one who gives life to all the beings on this world. You are the physician who cures the fever to the life and death cycles of the wheel of life. You are the source of life and liberation of all living beings. We pray to that tireless energy which resides as Mother Goddess in Haidakhan. Remembering you is to crown this life with success, to attain liberation.

O, Mother, yours is the ultimate form. You are ever-present in everything existent; You are the Universal Mother in all eternity. Giver of all that is good. Great yogis meditate at your lotus feet. As the benefactress of the universe, you maintain absolute truth.

O Durga, unattainable goddess, you kill disease and every kind of evil, destroying all darkness and taking away the sorrows of this world. Shining with the effulgence of the sun. You are worshipped as Tara, she who guides the souls. Repeating this name helps your worshipper to cross the sea of life with ease.

You are omnipresent and all knowing. Your divine law is imprinted on every atom. You are the giver of divine perfection according to your own sweet will. You are the form of every source of knowledge, of all science, the giver of worldly pleasures and of liberation of the soul. To you we bow.

Only you can give liberation to the beings of this world, O Devi, who sustains and cares for all creation, being above the three qualities of life. The mind cannot conceive you, nor can the world describe your deep mysterious being. This is why by worshipping you alone the creatures of the world obtain fulfillment of all they desire. O Mother, we bow to you.

You are supreme knowledge. Your form is eternal everlasting peace. You are the ultimate root of all the elements. Your form is bound to mercy; the one on whom you bestow your grace has the great fortune of receiving your darshan and with it great happiness. O goddess of abundance, to you we bow.

Salutations to you, Mother of the universes; we bow to you who lives in them forever—through all the ages. Your form is beyond the decay of time; inherent in everything. You are immortal. You are beyond being known, of unfathomable mystery. Great Mother, we bow to you.

O Devi, You are prosperity and the power of increase. To you we bow. You are radiant light; we bow to You. Benefactress of the world. The whole universe is full of your glory. You are the pure nectar essence of all images made in Your likeness. To You we bow, O Goddess.

You bestow happiness on all the universes and shower grace on Your devotees and give them nourishment in plenty. You are radiant with divine effulgence. You are the one who takes away all troubles and You annihilate all fear. To You the supreme energy we bow again and again.

You always reside in the heart of all beings as their own self. As Maya, the cosmic illusion, You adorn life with the most beautiful glow; You are ever-perfect in Your divinity as supreme knowledge; You are the ultimate point in the infinity of cosmic space! As the universal self, You shower the rain of divine nectar on the world and let the rain of bliss drown all the fears of this world. O Mother, we seek refuge in You.

You are compassion and forgiveness, modesty and all longing. You are the brilliance, peace and life energy in human beings. You are the beauty of knowledge. You are the energy that gives vision to the eyes. You are mind and speech and in the senses. You are the receptive and creative capacity. All these different aspects of energy are there because of Your power.

O Mahalaksmi, goddess of great magnificence, Your eyes have the beauty of the lotus; come and bless me with one glance of mercy and give an Initiation. O Mother, You clear the path of obstacles of him who has obtained Your mercy. You are the fount of true knowledge and grant boons to him who is under Your protection. O Sarvesvari, protect me!

O Mother, You and the luminosity of the moon and the sun's divine light is Yours; even the pure radiance of your planets is a reflection of You. You are the fire's ardour and the softness of water, the strength in the earth; Yours is the Power to sustain

183

the earth. Yours is the Power in the universe and it is You who is the preserving energy.

O Mother, just as there is no one who can count the jewels in the deep seas, there is no one who has the gift of words to describe adequately the glory of the sun, and can recount the wondrous lilas that have been Yours since the time of creation. You appear like the full moon from a sea of bliss and consciousness, radiant with divine brilliance.

Hymn of Worship to the Mother

O Divine Mother, happily residing in Haidakhan
You tend to all beings of the universe
O great Goddess, abounding with grace
Glory be to you, O mother of the universe
Energy of Shiva the Lord

You dispel the darkness of the world
You bestow knowledge;
Your being is wholly light
Glory be to you

You destroy the pain, illusions, and fear of this world
You eliminate all obstacles on the path to perfection
Your heart melts with divine love
Glory be to you

In the ocean of this life there swim
Like crocodiles six enemies
(anger, greed, ego, fear, lust, attachment)
You make us cross the ocean, O Mother;
Many you have guided across, so help us too.
Glory be to you

You help overcome attachment, envy, and pride
You liberate the whole world
You are the invisible energy of the Lord
Glory be to you

You are the seed and the power of the word
You shine with divine light
You are the all-embracing life energy
Glory be to you

Focusing on the Divine Mother now will soften our hearts. It will make us more affectionate to the children of the world and stimulate us to fill ourselves with more kindness, tenderness, cooperation, and encouragement in our relationships. It will help us to be filled with universal love. Developing the motherly aspect of God will help us feel love for all people in the world.

Try reading the names of the Mother and these prayers daily and see what happens. Meditate on the Mother who can give you true blessing.

GIFT OF THE DIVINE MOTHER
By Kate Nelson

I bow and in bowing
    Kiss the earth of the Divine Mother
I sit and in sitting
    Receive the grace of the Divine Mother
I stand and in standing
    Reflect the light of the Divine Mother
I walk and in walking
    Follow the path of the Divine Mother
I see and in seeing
    Behold the glory of the Divine Mother
I listen and in listening
    Hear the song of the Divine Mother
I pray and in praying
    Enter into the presence of the Divine Mother
I am and in being
    Become one with the Divine Mother.

13

DIVINE LESSONS FROM AMMA

Holy Mother Amritanandamayi is esteemed as a stupendous incarnation of the Divine Mother herself. Today she is India's leading female light. She selflessly travels the world to console, hug, heal, and inspire her millions of children with the power of divine love. I am one of these fortunate children, and I have no word to express the inner joy I feel when just thinking of her. She takes into her lap thousands of people every day, of all ages, religions, races, and walks of life. She absorbs their suffering and negativity into her own body. She blesses us all and heals us all with her gentle caresses.

It has been said that "The lady of love, simply known as 'Amma,' may be the greatest phenomenon in the history of religion." I agree that she certainly has emerged as one of the most powerful spiritual masters ever to walk the planet. Although she was a child prodigy, she had a difficult childhood. But she was walking and speaking at six months and singing to Lord Krishna right away.

Her presence is always a potent blessing force, opening us up and infusing our spiritual energy centers. Her body vibrates with tremendous power (shakti) of divine love. It is as though she is connected to an electrical current that supercharges her biological structure.

She is a living fountain of grace, and I feel incredulous at my good fortune of having been able to be near her divinity in human form. Go on her website, Amma.org, and see when her schedule will take her near you. Many consider her to be like a female Christ who always helps release us from old wounds and karmic bonds and awakens us to divine spirit. Why miss this chance? People have seen her levitate and bilocate. She is like a female form of Babaji also. One friend I took leaned over and whispered to me at 3 AM, "This is the highest thing there is on the whole planet." I said, "Ohhh . . . I am so glad you feel that way!" He then said, "Well it is the Source!" It was his first time with Amma. So you see, God herself is appearing in our midst!

Here are some of Amma's observations:

The moment of revelation that has occurred to many great souls can happen to you as well. Everybody is being prepared to reach this final

188

state of dropping all worldly attachments, all ego. It must happen because that is the final stage of evolution. You cannot avoid it. . . . The final destiny for all souls is the dropping away of every obstruction to peace and contentment. When that moment comes, the ego is dropped and you won't struggle anymore. . . . You will just bow down and surrender.

Each one of you has the beauty and power of a saint or sage. Each one of you is an infinite source of power. Yet when you see a saint or sage, you recoil. Saying "No this is for those special people. I can't do it. I have my own tiny little world to bother about, and that's enough for me. Divinity is none of my business. . . ." This kind of attitude will never help you to come out of the small, hard shell of your little ego. . . . That is why the Vedanta tells us to contemplate the Veida distum. "I am Brahman (Absolute Reality). I am God. I am the Universe. I am absolute Power, the totality of consciousness, which makes everything beautiful and full of light and life."

When somebody insults you, he is insulting you from his past, and when you react you, too, are reacting from the past. Both of you have been victims of insults and have made others your victims in your previous lifetimes as well as in this lifetime. . . . When others insult you or get angry at you, try to keep your mouth shut, imagining that you are in Amma's presence. . . . Try to feel respect for the other person, because in truth, he is doing something good for you. He is teaching you to be silent, to be patient. . . . Feel deep concern and compassion for him. . . . Try to see that your accuser is suffering from his past wounds. You do not want to hurt a wounded and suffering person. That is cruelty. Be kind and compassionate.

You can raise a hundred objections to the theory of karma . . . Still the law of karma is operating in your life. You are in its grip. Children, our actions will return to each one of us, whether one is a believer or non believer. Karma is like a boomerang. Newborn babies are physically deformed or mentally retarded. Are such events accidental? No! Each thing that happens in life has a cause. Sometimes the cause is visible and at other times it is not. Sometimes the cause is to be found in the immediate past, but in some cases it stems from the remote past. . . . Nothing is accidental. Nature is not accidental. Creation is not an accident. Our past in not just the past of this lifetime. The past is also all the previous lifetimes through which we have traveled in different names and forms. We must be alert and careful about what we do today because we do not know what effect it will produce tomorrow. Your negative feelings will invoke the negative feeling in others. They too will suffer, thereby adding to the storehouse of their karma. Thus through your anger or selfishness, you have lengthened the chain of someone else's karma also. You are responsible since it happens due to your anger and greed. This is the kind of destruction you do.

Contentment ensues from egolessness. And egolessness comes from devotion, love, and utter surrender to the Supreme Lord. An ordinary devotee wants to keep his ego, whereas a true devotee wants to die to his ego so that he can live in consciousness of pure innocent love. Dying to the ego . . . makes you immortal. Death of the ego leads you to deathlessness. When the ego dies, you live eternally in bliss.

"THE AWAKENING OF UNIVERSAL MOTHERHOOD"

The following is an address given by Her Holiness Sri Mata Amritanandamayi on the occasion of A Global Peace Initiative of Women Religious and Spiritual Leaders, in Palais des Nations, Geneva, on October 7, 2002:

Women are the power and the very foundation of our existence in the world. It is therefore crucial that women everywhere make every effort to rediscover their fundamental nature, for only then can we save this world.

Amma bows down to all of you who are truly the embodiments of supreme consciousness and love.

Women and men are equal in Amma's eyes. Amma wants to honestly express her views on this very subject. These observations don't necessarily apply to everyone, but they do apply to the majority of people.

At present, most women are asleep. Women have to wake up and arise. This is one of the most urgent needs of the age. Not only should women living in developing countries wake up—this applies to women all over the world. Women in countries where materialism is predominant should awaken to spirituality.[1] And women in countries where they

---

[1] The spirituality that Amma refers to here is not about worshipping a God sitting somewhere up about the clouds. Real spirituality is to know oneself

are forced to remain inside the narrow walls of religious tradition should awaken to modern thinking. It has been widely believed that women and the cultures in which they live will awaken through education and material development. But time has taught us that this concept is too limited. Only when women imbibe the eternal wisdom of spirituality, along with modern education, will the power within them awaken—and they will rise to action.

Who should awaken woman? What obstructs her awakening? In truth, no external power can possibly obstruct woman or her innate qualities of motherhood—qualities such as love, empathy, and patience. It is she—she alone—who has to awaken herself. A woman's mind is the only real barrier that prevents this from happening.

The rules and superstitious beliefs that degrade women continue to prevail in most countries. The primitive customs invented by men in the past to exploit and to subjugate women remain alive to this day. Women and their minds have become entangled in the cobweb of those customs. They have been hypnotized by their own minds. Women have to help themselves in order to extricate themselves from that magnetic field. This is the only way.

---

and to realize the infinite Power within. Spirituality and life are not two separate things; they are one. Real spirituality teaches us how to live in the world. Material science teaches us how to air-condition the external world, whereas spiritual science teaches us how to air-condition the internal world.

Look at an elephant. It can uproot huge trees with its trunk. When an elephant living in captivity is still a baby, it is tied to a tree with a strong rope or a chain. Because it is the nature of elephants to roam free, the baby elephant instinctively tries with all its might to break the rope. But it isn't strong enough to do so. Realizing its efforts are of no use, it finally gives up and stops struggling. Later, when the elephant is fully grown, it can be tied to a small tree with a thin rope. It could then easily free itself by uprooting the tree and breaking the rope. But because his mind has been conditioned by its prior experiences, it doesn't make the slightest attempt to break free.

That is what is happening to women.

Society does not allow the strength of women to arise. We have created a blockage, preventing this great strength from flowing out.

The infinite potential inherent in women and men is the same. If women really want to, it won't be difficult to break the shackles—the rules and conditioning that society has imposed on them. The greatest strength of women lies in their innate motherhood, in their creative, life-giving power. And this power can help women to bring about a far more significant change in society than men could ever accomplish.

Antiquated, crippling concepts devised in the past are blocking women from reaching spiritual heights. Those are the shadows that still haunt women, evoking fear and distrust within. Women should let go of their fear and distrust—they are simply illusions. The limitations women think they have are not real. Women need to muster the strength to overcome those imagined limitations. They already possess this power; it is right here! And once that power has been evoked, no one will be able to stop the forward march of women in every area of life.

Men normally believe in muscle power. On a superficial level they see women as their mothers, wives, and sisters. But there is no need to hide the fact that, on a deeper level, men still have a great deal of resistance when it comes to properly understanding, accepting, and recognizing women and the feminine aspect of life.

Amma remembers a story. In a village there lived a deeply spiritual woman who found immense happiness in serving others. The religious leaders of the village chose her as one of their priests. She was the first appointed woman priest, and the male priests didn't like it one bit. Her great compassion, humility, and wisdom were appreciated by the villagers. This caused a lot of jealousy among the male priests.

One day all the priests were invited to a religious gathering on an island, three hours away by boat. As the priests boarded the boat they discovered, to their dismay that the woman priest was already seated inside. They muttered among themselves, "What a pain! She just won't leave us alone!" The boat set off. But an hour later the engine suddenly died and the boat came to a standstill! The captain exclaimed, "Oh no! We're stuck! I forgot to fill the tank!" Nobody knew what to do. There was no other boat in sight. At this point the woman priest stood up and said, "Don't worry, brothers! I'll go and fetch more fuel." Having said this, she stepped out of the boat and proceeded to walk away across the water. The priests watched with great astonishment, but were quick to remark, "Look at her! She doesn't even know how to swim!"

This is the attitude of men in general. It lies in their nature to belittle and condemn the achievements of women. Women are not decorations or objects meant to be controlled by men. Men treat women like potted plants, making it impossible for them to grow to their full potential.

Women were not created for the enjoyment of men. They were not made to host tea parties. Men use women like a tape recorder, which they like to control according to their whims and fancies, as if they were pressing play and pause buttons.

Men consider themselves superior to women, both physically and intellectually. The arrogance of men's mistaken attitude—that women cannot survive in society without depending on men—is obvious in everything that men do.

If a woman's character is considered flawed, even if she is an innocent victim, she will be rejected by society and often by her family. Whereas, a man can be as immoral as he likes and get away with it. He is seldom questioned.

Even in materially developed countries, women are pushed back when it comes to sharing political power with men. It is interesting to see that, compared to developed countries, developing countries are far ahead in providing opportunities for women to rise in politics. But, except for a few who can be counted on one's fingers, how many women can be seen in the arena of world politics? Is it this way because women are incapable, or is it due to the arrogance of men?

The right circumstances and support of others will certainly help women to awaken and arise. But this alone is not enough. They need to draw inspiration from those circumstances and find strength within themselves. Real power and strength do not come from the outside; they are to be found within.

Women have to find their courage. Courage is an attribute of the mind; it is not a quality of the body. Women have the power to fight against the social rules that prevent their progress. This is Amma's own experience, although a lot of changes have taken place, India is a country where male supremacy is still the rule. Even today, women are exploited in the name of religious convention and tradition. In India, too, women are walking up and springing into action. Until recently, women were not allowed to worship in the inner sanctum of a temple, nor could women consecrate a temple or perform Vedic rituals. Women didn't even have the freedom to chant Vedic mantras. But Amma is encouraging and appointing women to do these things. And it is Amma who performs the consecration ceremony in all the temples built by our ashram. There were many who protested against women doing these things, because for generations all those ceremonies and rituals had been done only by men. To those who questioned what we were doing, Amma explained that we are worshipping a God who is beyond all differences, who does not differentiate between male and female. As it turns out, the majority of people have supported this revolutionary move. Those prohibitions against women were never actually a part of ancient Hindu tradition. They were in all likelihood invented later by men who belonged to the higher classes of society, in order to exploit and oppress women. They didn't exist in ancient India.

In ancient India, the Sanskrit words that a husband used when addressing his wife were *Pathni*—the one who leads the husband through life; *Dharmapathni*—the one who guides her husband on the path of dharma [righteousness and responsibility]; and *Sahadharmacharini*—the one who moves together with her husband on the path of *dharma*. These terms imply that women enjoyed the same status as men, or perhaps an even higher one. Married life was considered sacred, for it lived with the right attitude and right understanding. With both husband and wife supporting each other, it would lead them to the ultimate goal of life—Self-realization of God-realization.

In India, the supreme being has never been worshipped exclusively in a masculine form. The supreme being is also worshipped as the Goddess in her many aspects. She is, for example, worshipped as Saraswati, the goddess of wisdom and leaning; she is worshipped as Lakshmi, the goddess of prosperity; and Santana Lakshmi, the goddess who gives new life within a woman. She is also worshipped as Durga, the Goddess of strength and power. There was a time when men revered woman as the embodiment of these very qualities. She was considered an extension of the Goddess, and manifestation of her attributes on Earth. And then, at some point, because of the selfishness of certain men of influence and their desire for power and dominion over all, this deep truth was distorted and severed from our culture. And thus it was that people forgot or ignored that profound connection between woman and the Divine Mother.

It is commonly believe that the religion that gives least status to women is Islam. But the Koran speaks of qualities such as compassion and wisdom, and of God's essential nature, as feminine.

In Christianity, the supreme being is worshipped exclusively as the Father in heaven, the Son, and the Holy Ghost. The feminine aspect of God is not so widely recognized. Christ considered men and women equal.

For Christ, Krishna, and Buddha to be born, a woman was needed. In order to incarnate, God needed a woman, who went through all the pain and hardship of pregnancy and giving birth. A man was not capable of this. Yet no one considers the injustice of women being ruled by men. No genuine religion will look down upon women or speak of women in a derogatory manner.

For those who have realized God, there is no difference between male and female. The realized ones have equal vision. If anywhere in the world there exists rules that prevent women from enjoying their rightful freedom, rules that obstruct their progress in society, then those are not God's commandments, but are born out of the selfishness of men.

Which eye is more important, the left or the right? Both are equally important. It is the same with the status of men and women in society. Both should be aware of their unique responsibilities, or dharma. Men and women have to support one another. Only in this way can we maintain the harmony of the world. When men and women become powers that complement each other, and move together with cooperation and mutual respect, they will attain perfection.

In reality, men are a part of women. Every child first lies in the mother's womb, as a part of the woman's very being. As far as a birth is concerned, a man's only role is to offer his seed. For him it is only a moment of pleasure; for a woman it is nine months of austerities. It is the woman who receives, conceives, and makes that life a part of her being. She creates the most conducive atmosphere for that life to grow within her and then gives birth to that life. Women are essentially mothers, the creators of life. There is a hidden longing in all men to be reenfolded by the unconditional love of a mother. This is one of the subtle reasons for the attraction that men feel towards women—because a man is out of a woman.

No one can question the reality of motherhood—that men are created from women. Yet those who refuse to come out of the cocoon of their narrow minds will never be able to understand. You cannot explain light to those who know only darkness.

The principle of motherhood is as vast and powerful as the universe. With the power of motherhood within her, a woman can influence the entire world.

Is God a man or a woman? The answer to that question is that God is neither male nor female—God is "That." But if you insist of god having a gender, then God is more female than male, because the masculine is contained within the feminine.

Anyone—woman or man—who has the courage to overcome the limitations of the mind can attain the state of universal motherhood. The love of awakened motherhood is a love and compassion felt, not only towards one's own children, but towards all people, animals and plants, rocks and rivers—a love extended to all of nature, all beings. Indeed, to a woman in whom the state of true motherhood has awakened, all creatures are her children. This love, this motherhood, is divine love—and that is God.

More than half of the world's population is women. It is a great loss when women are denied the freedom to come forward, and when they are denied the high status that should be theirs in society. When women are denied this, society loses their potential contribution.

When women are undermined, their children become weak as well. In this way, a whole generation loses its strength and vitality. Only when women are accorded the honour they deserve, can we create a world of light and awareness.

Women can perform all tasks just as well as men—perhaps even better. Women have the willpower and creative energy to do any type of work. Amma can say this based on her own experience. Whatever the form of action, women can attain extraordinary heights, and this is true especially on the spiritual path. Women have the purity of mind and intellectual capacity to achieve this. But, whatever they undertake, the beginning should be positive. If the beginning is good, the middle and the end will automatically be good, provided one has patience, faith, and love. A wrong beginning set on family foundations is one of the reasons why women lose out so much in life. It isn't only that women should share equal status with men in society, the problem is that women are given a bad start in life, due to wrong understanding and lack of proper awareness. So, women are trying to reach the end without the benefit of having the beginning.

If we want to learn to read the Roman alphabet, we have to begin with ABC, not with XYZ. And what is the ABC of women? What is the very fiber of a woman's being, her existence? It is her inborn qualities, the essential principles of motherhood. Whatever area of work a woman chooses, she shouldn't forget these virtues that God or Nature has graciously bestowed on her. A woman should perform all her actions being firmly rooted in the very ground of these qualities. Just as ABC is the beginning of the alphabet, the quality of motherhood is the foundation of a woman. She shouldn't leave out that crucial part of herself before she moves on to other levels.

There are many powers in women that are generally not found in men. A woman has the ability to divide herself into many. Contrary to men, women have the capacity to do several things at the same time. Even if she has to divide herself, and do many different things simultaneously, a woman is gifted with the ability to carry out all actions with great beauty and perfection. Even in her role as a mother, a woman is able to bring forth many different facets of her being—she has to be warm and tender, strong and protective, and a strict disciplinarian. Rarely do we see this kind of confluence of qualities in men. So, in fact, women have a greater responsibility than men. Women hold the reins of integrity and unity in the family and in society.

A man's mind easily becomes identified with his thoughts and actions. Male energy can be compared to stagnant water; it doesn't flow. The mind and intellect of a man usually get stuck in the work that he does. It is difficult for men to shift their minds from one focus to another. Because of this, the professional life and family life of many men become mixed up. Most men cannot separate the two. Women, on the other hand, have an inborn capacity to do this. It is a deep-rooted tendency of a man to bring his professional persona home and behave accordingly in his relationship with his wife and children. Most women know how to keep their family life and professional life separate.

Feminine energy, or a woman's energy, is fluid like a river. This makes it easy for a woman to be a mother, a wife, and a good friend who provides her husband with confidence. She has the special gift to be the guide and advisor of the entire family. Women who have jobs are more than capable of succeeding in that as well.

The power of a woman's innate motherhood helps her to find a deep sense of peace and harmony within herself. This enables her to reflect less and react more. A woman can listen to the sorrows of other people and respond with compassion; but, still, when faced with a challenge, she can rise to the situation and react as strongly as any man.

In today's world, everything is being contaminated and made unnatural. In this environment, woman should take extra care that her qualities of motherhood—her essential nature as a woman—don't become contaminated and distorted.

There is a man in the inner depths of every woman, and a woman in the inner depths of every man. This truth dawned in the meditation of the great saints and seers eons ago. This is what the Ardhanariswara (half-God and half-Goddess) concept in the Hindu faith signifies. Whether you are a woman or a man, your real humanity will come to light only when the feminine and masculine qualities within you are balanced.

Men have also suffered greatly as a result of the exile of the feminine principle from the world. Because of the oppression of women and the suppression of the feminine aspect within men, men's lives have become fragmented, often painful. Men, too, have to awaken to their feminine qualities. They have to develop empathy and understanding in their attitude toward women, and in the way they relate to the world.

Statistics show that men—not women—commit by far most of the crime and murder in this world. There is also a deep connection between the way men destroy Mother Nature and their attitude towards women. Nature should be accorded the same importance in our hearts as our own biological mothers.

Only love, compassion, and patience—the fundamental qualities of women—can lessen the intrinsically aggressive, overactive tendencies of men. Similarly, there are women who need the qualities of men, so that their good and gentle nature doesn't immobilize them.

Women are the power and the very foundation of our existence in the world. When women lose touch with their real selves, the harmony of the world ceases to exist, and destruction sets in. It is therefore crucial that women everywhere make every effort to rediscover their fundamental nature, for only then can we save this world.

What today's world really needs is cooperation between men and women, based on a firm sense of unity in the family and society. Wars and conflicts, all the suffering and lack of peace in the present-day world, will certainly lessen to a great extent if women and men begin to cooperate and to support each other. Unless harmony is restored between the masculine and the feminine, between men and women, peace will continue to be no more than a distant dream.

There are two types of language in the world: the language of the intellect and the language of the heart. The language of the dry, rational intellect likes to argue and attack. Aggression is its nature. It is purely masculine, devoid of love or any sense of relatedness. It says, "Not only am I right and you are wrong, but I have to prove this at all costs so that you will yield to me." Controlling others and making them puppets that dance according to their tune is typical of those who speak this language. They try to force their ideas on others. Their hearts are closed. They rarely consider anyone else's feelings. Their only consideration is their own ego and their hollow idea of victory.

The language of the heart, the language of love, which is related to the feminine principle, is quite different. Those who speak this language do not care about their ego. They have no interest in proving that they are right or that anyone else is wrong. They are deeply concerned about their fellow beings and wish to help, support, and uplift others. In their presence transformation simply happens. They are the givers of tangible hope and of light in this world. Those who approach them are reborn. When such people speak it is not to lecture, to impress, or to argue—it is a true communion of hearts.

Real love has nothing to do with lust or self-centeredness. In real love, you are not important; the other is important. In love, the other is not your instrument to fulfill your selfish desires; you are an instrument of the Divine with the intention of doing good in the world. Love does not sacrifice others; love gives joyfully of itself. Love is selfless—but not the enforced selflessness of women being pushed into the background, treated as objects. In real love, you do not feel worthless; on the contrary, you expand and become one with everything—all-encompassing, ever blissful.

Unfortunately, in today's world, it is the language of the intellect that prevails, not the language of the heart. Selfishness and the eyes of lust—not love—dominate the world. Narrow-minded people influence those with weaker minds and use them to fulfill their selfish goals. The ancient teachings of the sages have been distorted to fit within the narrow frames of men's selfish desires. The concept of love has been distorted. This is why the world is filled with conflicts, violence, and war.

Woman is the creator of the human race. She is the first Guru, the first guide and mentor of humanity. Think of the tremendous forces, either positive or negative, that one human being can unleash upon the world. Each one of us has a far-reaching effect on others, whether we are aware of it or not. The responsibility of a mother, when it comes to influencing and inspiring her children, cannot be underestimated. There is much truth in the saying that there is a strong woman behind every successful man. Wherever you see happy, peaceful individuals; wherever you see children endowed with noble qualities and good dispositions; wherever you see men who have immense strength when faced with failure and adverse situations; wherever you see people who possess a great measure of understanding, sympathy, love, and compassion towards the suffering, and who give themselves to others—you will usually find a great mother who has inspired them to become what they are.

Mothers are the ones who are most able to sow the seeds of love, universal kinship, and patience in the minds of human beings. There is a special bond between a mother and child. The mother's inner qualities are transmitted to the child even through her breast milk. The mother understands the heart of her child; she pours her love into the child, teaches him or her the positive lessons of life, and corrects the child's mistakes. If you walk through a field of soft, green grass a few times, you will easily make a path. The good thoughts and positive values we cultivate in our children will stay with them forever. It is easy to mold a child's character when he or she is very young, and much more difficult to do so when the child grows up.

Once, when Amma was giving darshan in India, a youth came up to her. He lived in a part of the country that was ravaged by terrorism. Because of the frequent killings and lootings, the people in that area were suffering a great deal. He told Amma that he was the leader of a group of youngsters who were doing a lot of social work in that area. He prayed to Amma, "Please give those terrorists, who are so full of hatred and violence, the right understanding. And for all those who have faced so many atrocities and have suffered so much, please fill their hearts with the spirit of forgiveness. Otherwise, the situation will only deteriorate, and there will be no end to the violence."

Amma was so glad to hear his prayer for peace and

forgiveness. When Amma asked him what made him choose a life of social work, he said, "My mother was the inspiration behind this. My childhood days were dark and terrifying. When I was six years old, I watched with my own eyes as my peace-loving father was brutally murdered by terrorists. My life was shattered. I was filled with hatred, and all I wanted was revenge. But my mother changed my attitude. Whenever I would tell her that I was going to avenge my father's death one day, she would say, 'Son, will your father come back to life if you kill those people? Look at your grandmother, how sad she always is. Look at me, how difficult it is to make ends meet without your father. And just look at yourself, how sad you are, not having your father with you. Would you want more mothers and children to suffer as we do? The intensity of this pain would be the same for them. Try to forgive your father's killers for their terrible deeds, and spread the message of love and universal kinship instead.' When I grew up, people tried to get me to join different terrorist outfits to avenge my father's death. But the seeds of forgiveness sown by my mother had borne fruit, and I refused. I gave some of the youngsters the same advice that my mother had given me. This changed the hearts of many people who have since joined me in serving others."

The love and compassion, rather than hatred, that this boy chose to pour into the world, stemmed from the wellspring of love in his mother.

It is thus, through the influence she has on her child, that a mother influences the future of the world. A woman who has awakened her innate motherhood brings heaven to earth wherever she is. Only women can create a peaceful, happy world. And so it is that the one who rocks the cradle of the babe is the one who holds up the lamp, shedding light upon the world.

Men should never hinder a woman's progress towards her rightful position in society. They should understand that the full contribution of women to the world is vitally important. Men should move out of her path; nay, they should prepare her path, to make her forward movement smoother.

A woman, for her part, should think of what she can give to society, rather than what she can take. This attitude will certainly help her to progress. It should be underscored that a woman doesn't need to receive or to take anything from anyone. She simply needs to awaken. Then she will be able to contribute whatever she wishes to give to society, and she will gain everything she needs.

Rather than becoming rusty, living out their lives inside the four walls of the kitchen, women should come out and share with others what they have to give, and fulfill their goals in life. Today, when competition and anger are the norm everywhere, it is the patience and tolerance of women that create whatever harmony there is in the world. Just as a complete electrical circuit depends on the presence of both positive and negative poles, life flowing in all its fullness depends on the presence and contribution of women as well as of men. Only when women and men complement and support each other will their inner blossoming take place.

In general, today's women are living in a world fashioned by and for men. Women have no need of that world; they should establish their own identities, and thus recreate society. But they should remember the real meaning of freedom. It is not a license to live and behave any way one likes, regardless of the consequences for others; it doesn't mean that wives and mothers should run away from their family responsibilities. A woman's freedom and rising has to begin within herself. Also, for shakti, or pure power, to awaken and arise in a woman, she first has to become aware of her weaknesses. She can then overcome those weaknesses through her willpower, selfless service, and spiritual practice.

In the process of striving to regain their rightful position in society, women should never lose their essential nature. This tendency can be seen in many countries, and will never help women to achieve true freedom. It is impossible to attain real freedom by imitating men. If women themselves turn their backs on the feminine principle, this will culminate in the utter failure of women and society. Then the problems of the world will not be resolved, but only aggravated. If women reject their feminine qualities and try to become like men, cultivating only masculine qualities, the imbalance in the world will only become greater. This is not the need of the age. The real need is for women to contribute all they can to society by developing their universal motherhood, as well as their masculine qualities.

As long as women do not make the effort to awaken, they are, in a way, themselves responsible for creating their own narrow world.

The more a woman identifies with her inner motherhood, the more she awakens to that shakti, or pure power. When women develop this power within themselves, the world will begin to listen to their voices more and more.

Many commendable individuals and organizations, like the UN, are supporting the progress of women. This conference is an opportunity for us to build on that foundation. Amma would like to share a few suggestions:

1. Religious leaders should make every effort to guide their followers back to the true essence of spirituality, and in light of this, condemn all types of oppression and violence against women.

2. The UN should go in and provide safe havens for women and children in war zones and areas of communal strife where they are particularly targeted.

3. All religions and nations should condemn such shameful practices as female feticide and infanticide, and female genital mutilation.

4. Child labour should be stopped.

5. The dowry system should be abolished.

6. The UN and leaders of every nation should intensify their efforts to stop child trafficking and the sexual exploitation of young girls. The legal consequences of such behavior should be effective deterrents.

7. The number of rapes taking place all over the world is astounding. And the fact that in some countries it is the victims of rape who are punished is incomprehensible. Can we merely stand by and watch this? There should be a concerted, international effort to educate young men, with the aim of putting an end to rape and other forms of violence against women.

8. The dignity of women is assailed by advertisements that treat them as sex objects. We should not tolerate this exploitation.

9. Religious leaders should encourage their followers to make selfless service an integral part of their lives.

The essence of motherhood is not restricted to women who have given birth; it is a principle inherent in both women and men. It is an attitude of the mind. It is love—and that love is the very breath of life. No one would say, "I will breathe only when I am with my family and friends; I won't breathe in front of my enemies." Similarly, for those in whom motherhood has awakened, love and compassion for everyone is as much part of their being as breathing.

Amma feels that the forthcoming age should be dedicated to reawakening the healing power of motherhood. This is the only way to realize our dream of peace and harmony for all. And it can be done! It is entirely up to us. Let us remember this and move forward.

Amma would like to thank all those involved in organizing this summit. Amma deeply honours your efforts to bring peace to this world. May the seeds of peace we are planting here today bear fruit for all.

An Interview with Mata Amritanandamayi

"When You Go Beyond the Ego You Become an Offering to the World," by Amy Edelstein (from *What Is Enlightenment?* magazine, issue 17/Spring–Summer 2000).

WIE: What is the role of the spiritual master in guiding the seeker on the path to *moksha*, or liberation?

MA: If you want to learn how to drive, you need to be taught by an experienced driver. A child needs to be taught how to tie his shoelaces. And how can you learn mathematics without a teacher? Even a pickpocket needs a teacher to teach him the art of stealing. If teachers are indispensable in ordinary life, wouldn't we need a teacher even more on the spiritual path, which is so extremely subtle?

Though that subtle knowledge is our true nature, we have been identified with the world of names and forms for so long, thinking them to be real. We now need to cease that identification. But in reality, there is nothing to teach. A master simply helps you to complete the journey.

If you want to go to a distant place, you may want to buy a map. But no matter how well you study the map, if you are heading toward a totally strange land, an unknown place, you won't know anything about the place until you actually arrive. Nor will the map tell you much about the journey itself, about the ups and downs of the road and the possible dangers on the way. It is therefore better to receive guidance from someone who has completed the journey, someone who knows that way from his or her own experience.

On the spiritual journey, we have to really listen to and then contemplate what the master says. We have to be humble in order to receive. When we really listen and then sincerely contemplate, we will assimilate the teachings properly.

WIE: Why is submission to a guru said to be so important in helping a disciple transcend the ego?

MA: The seat of the ego is the mind. Any other obstacle can be removed by using the mind except the ego, because the ego is subtler than the mind. It is only through obedience to the one who is established in that supreme experience that one can conquer the ego.

WIE: You didn't have an external guru, yet you completely transcended your ego. It seems you depended on the form-less as your guru to take you all the way.

MA: Yes, you could say that. But Amma considered the whole of creation to be her guru.

WIE: Is perfect obedience to the guru ultimately the same as ego death?

MA: Yes. That is why the *satguru* [realized spiritual master]

is depicted in the Kathopanishad as Yama, the lord of death. The death of the disciple's ego can take place only with the help of a satguru.

Obedience isn't something that can be forced on the disciple. The disciple is tremendously inspired by the master, who is an embodiment of humility. Obedience and humility simply happen in a true master's presence.

WIE: It takes rare courage to face ego death.

MA: Yes, very few can do it. If you have the courage and determination to knock at the door of death, you will find that there is not death. For even death, or the death of the ego, is an illusion.

WIE: There have been some very powerful spiritual teachers who seem to have been driven by the impure motives of the ego. Do you think that spiritual experiences could at times empower the ego rather than destroy it?

MA: Amma doesn't agree that those teachers to whom you are referring are realized. A Self-realized master is completely independent. Such beings don't have to depend on anything external for their happiness because they are full of bliss, which they derive from within their own *Atman*. Amma would say that everyone forms part of a crowd, except the realized masters. In fact, except for those rare souls, there are no individuals. Only one who is realized is uniquely individual and totally independent of the crowd. Only such a soul is alone in the world of bliss.

True spiritual masters have to set an example through their actions and their lives. Those who abuse their position and power, taking advantage of others, obviously do not derive all their happiness and contentment from within themselves, and so they cannot be realized masters. Why would a realized master crave adulation or power? Those who do are still under the grip of the ego. They may claim to be realized, but they are not. A perfect master doesn't claim anything. He simply *is*—he is *presence*.

Until the moment before realization takes place, a person is not safe from the temptations of his or her desires.

WIE: So would you say that people like this have become more proud as a result of having had spiritual experiences? Can spiritual experiences at times strengthen the ego in a negative way?

MA: The people to whom this happens are deluded, and they confuse others as well. They will actually push others into delusion. Some people gain a glimpse of something, or have a spiritual experience, and then think they have attained moksha. Only someone who is not realized will think, "I am spiritual, I am realized," and this will create a strong, subtle ego. A subtle ego is more dangerous than a gross ego. Even the individuals themselves won't understand that the subtle ego is leading or motivating them, and this subtle ego will become part of their nature. Such people will do anything for name and fame.

Amma also feels that this kind of pride makes people lose their capacity to listen. And listening is extremely important on the spiritual path. A person who does not listen cannot be humble. And it is only when we are truly humble that the already existing pure Consciousness will be unfolded within us. Only one who is humbler than the humblest can be considered greater than the greatest.

WIE: Since it is possible for spiritual experiences to feed the ego, is it necessary to cultivate purity first?

MA: There is no need to get obsessed with purity. Focus on your dharma, performing it with the right attitude and with love. Then purity will follow.

WIE: What is *dharma*, in the way you are using it?

MA: By loving life with the right attitude and having the right understanding, we will know what the right thing to do is. And then, if we perform our dharma, purity will come.

WIE: How do we cultivate that kind of love?

MA: Love isn't something that can be cultivated—it's already within us in all its fullness. Life cannot exist without love; they are inseparable. Life and love are not two; they are one and the same. A little bit of the proper channeling of your energies will awaken the love within you.

You need to have a strong intent to reach the goal of liberation; you need to be focused on that goal. Then such qualities as love, patience, enthusiasm and optimism will spring forth within you. These qualities will work to help you attain your goal.

WIE: You are revered by so many as the embodiment of unconditional love, and you literally hug everyone who comes to you. But I have heard that you can also be very fierce with your students. How do these two very different methods of teaching go together?

MA: For Amma there are not two different methods; Amma has only one method, and that is love. That love manifests as patience and compassion. However, if a deer comes and eats the tender flower buds in your garden, you cannot be gentle with the deer and say softly, "Please, deer, don't eat the flowers." You have to shout at it and even wave a stick. It is sometimes necessary to show this type of mood in order to correct the disciple. Kali is the compassionate mother in her disciplining mood. But look into her eyes—there is no anger there.

Amma only disciplines those who have chosen to stay close to her, and she only does this when they are ready to be disciplined. A disciple is one who is willing to be disciplined.

The guru first binds the disciple with boundless, unconditional love so that when the disciple eventually is disciplined, he or she is aware of the presence of that love in all situations.

Amma helps her children to always be aware and alert. Love has many aspects. When Amma disciplines her children, she does this with the sole purpose of guiding them along the path to help them to fully blossom. This blossoming will happen only if a conducive atmosphere is created. It can never be forced. A true master does not force his or her disciples because pure consciousness cannot force anything. The master is like space, like the boundless sky, and space cannot hurt you. Only the ego can force and hurt. Amma will patiently continue to create opportunities for that inner opening, that blossoming, to take place within her children.

The guru-disciple relationship is the highest. The bond of love between the guru and *shishya* [disciple] is so powerful that one may sometimes feel there is no guru and no shishya—all sense of separation disappears.

WIE: What do you do when the ego takes hold of one of your disciples?

MA: Amma lovingly helps her children to realize the danger of being under the grip of the ego, and she shows them how to get out of it.

WIE: Some Western psychotherapists and spiritual teachers believe that we must develop strong egos before we seek ego transcendence. They say that most of us have weak or wounded egos as a result of the emotional and psychological traumas that we have suffered over the course of our lives, and they advocate various forms of therapy to help us build up our character, ego, and sense of individuality. You had quite a difficult childhood; you had to bear harsh treatment and even physical abuse, and yet you transcended your ego completely. Would you agree with these teachers that in the pursuit of enlightenment, we first need to build up the ego before we endeavor to transcend it?

MA: Most people are deeply wounded within some way, and those wounds have been caused by the past. Those wounds usually remain unhealed. They are wounds not only from this life but from previous lives as well, and no doctor or psychologist can heal them. A doctor or psychologist can help people to cope with life to a certain extent, in spite of those wounds, but they cannot actually heal them. They cannot penetrate deeply enough into their own minds to remove their own wounds, let alone penetrate deeply enough into the patient's mind. Only a true master, who is completely free from any limitations and who is beyond the mind, can penetrate into a person's mind and treat all those unhealed wounds with his or her infinite energy. Spiritual life, especially under the guidance of a satguru, does not weaken the psyche; it strengthens it.

The ultimate cause of all emotional wounds is our

separation from the Atman, from our true nature. It may be necessary for a person to go to a psychologist, and that is fine—but to put spirituality aside in order to first strengthen the ego is to perpetuate that sense of separation, and it will only lead to further suffering. What is the use in thinking, "I will go to the doctor as soon as I feel better"? To wait for either the inner or outer circumstances to be "just right" before we embark on the spiritual journey is like standing on the seashore waiting for the waves to completely subside before we jump into the ocean. This will never happen. Every moment of life is so utterly precious, such a rare opportunity. We should not waste it.

Thank you to *What Is Enlightenment?* magazine for permission to publish this.

APPENDIX I

BREASTS AND THE PREVENTION OF BREAST CANCER

I remember in nursing school I attended a lecture for doctors and nurses on the subject of breastfeeding. I was amazed to hear the speaker say that when a newborn baby sucks on his mother's breasts, the husband often gets jealous, and the solution is to suggest that the husband sucks on the other breast at the same time! I thought it was cool that this was discussed out in the open. At the time, I had no idea that I was deeply affected by the fact that I myself had not been breastfed. Later during rebirthing sessions, I found out that I had been devastated as a newborn that I could not be breastfed.

One can recall such preverbal moments in breathwork, but it took me years before this memory came up. I was in Berlin right after the wall came down, and everything had a terrible feeling of depletion. My lovely assistant in Germany happened to be an obstetrician and a rebirther, which was a huge miracle for me. So of course I asked her to rebirth me, and that is when the memory came up. I blurted out, "This

225

is unforgivable. I might as well be in the streets." I was shocked at how upset I got. I finally got the nerve to discuss this with my mother. She told me she had tried and it did not work, and she was just as upset as I was about it.

At one point we rebirthers did more studies on this issue, and we found out that lack of breastfeeding affects prosperity. (Milk is nourishment, and money is nourishment.) No breastfeeding equals *lack*. It seems that people who were breastfed are more prosperous. I also wondered if anyone had ever done a study to see if breast cancer is more prevalent in women who had never been breastfed, but I never did that study. I did start to wonder, then, why so many women got breast cancer. My own mother had it. Fortunately, she recovered more quickly than anyone in history, they said, and she lived a long life and did not die from that.

I found out that the death rate from cancer of the breast has not changed much—that the situation is *not* improving. I hesitate to even give the statistics because statistics can be like modern voodoo. You read it and start believing it and creating it. The only reason to look at the cause of this is to wake up in order to prevent it.

I cherish four books about the metaphysical causes of disease, so I will share with you what they say about breast cancer:

1. *Heal Your Body,* by Louise Hay, is one great book we have had for decades in America. She says that breast problems (cysts, lumps, soreness, mastitis) are probably caused by a refusal to nourish the self, by putting everyone else first, and exiencing overmothering, overprotection, and over-bearing attitudes.

   The new thought pattern that Hays prescribes for this is: I am important. I count. I now care for and nourish myself with joy. I allow others the freedom to be who they are. We are all safe and free.

2. *The Body Is the Barometer of the Soul,* by Annette Noontil, also says that breast cancer is caused from not nurturing yourself, from taking care of others before taking care of you.

3. *Permanent Healing,* by Daniel Coondrom of the school of Metaphysics in Missouri, says that breast problems come from holding on to the old identity as a female and that cysts and lumps are caused by resentment or resistance to using the feminine expression.

4. *The Karmic Laws of Disease,* by Dr. Douglas Baker, devotes an entire chapter to this topic. Baker goes as far as to say that there is a deep-seated karmic cause in the sense that all cancers derive from the diseases that resulted from the excesses of the Atlantean root race, as it struggled with the

progressive opening and controlling of the solar plexus chakra.

He says that in breast cancer, there is the inability of the heart chakra to accept the excessive output of energies from the solar plexus, as that center acts as a channel for emotional drives. This manifests in emotional blocks, inhibitions, and irritations that stimulate cancer in the region of the breast.

He goes on to explain that there may be innate shyness and embarrassment with the sexual act, even after years of married life. There may be a deep distaste for the marriage partner and sexual demands could be regarded with deep loathing. Reading or hearing about rape, while having deep sympathetic rapport for other women, could bring out more revulsion, which could actually overstimulate the physical and etheric tissue in the breast area.

Emotional insecurity, especially associated with the husband or breadwinner, can produce the same sort of effect, he states. He even goes on to say that a woman can feel polluted if she realizes she has married someone she does not like or who is inferior.

He feels that in years ahead science will prove that emotionally disciplined women are less inflicted with breast cancer. What he recommends as a preventive is participation in the highest forms of classical arts: theater, music, sculpting, and painting. Of course, he would recommend being on a spiritual path in which you practice regular spiritual purification techniques to handle emotion.

I know women who had their breast lumps dissolved in ashrams with the help of spiritual masters and healers with high enough spiritual energy. But the point is to get the message and prevent it. Are *you* one of those women not nurturing yourself and always taking care of others first? Pay attention.

Appendix 2

Menopause as a Miracle

When I hit menopause, it did not seem like a miracle to me at all, especially since it came upon me the same time my mother died. I had to keep saying to myself the *Course in Miracles* lesson: I am willing to see this differently.

A rebirther in Palm Springs named Janice was driving me around, and she enlightened me on the subject. She told me she learned the following from her African friends of Burkina Faso: Menopause is a time when a woman's creative energy for childbirth is transferred into spiritual creativity. Women there are reverently honored in menopause for having the insight and wisdom as befitting a shaman in her tribe.

In this West African country, the woman who goes through the ceremony is carried around for twelve to fourteen days by the tribe. The whole village is there. They wash her, dress her, and feed her. They put on her makeup. Janice had attended an evening seminar when her African friends picked out a woman in the audience who was entering menopause.

The group was asked to do a bowl ceremony, symbolizing the filling and emptying of the uterus. Each person took a full bowl of water and one by one poured it into an empty bowl. Then the woman entering menopause was asked to stand in the middle and do what she was let to do to celebrate herself. The whole thing was about the passing of energy from procreation to the spiritual realm.

In my own case, getting through menopause felt really hard, and I could have used some inspiration such as that ceremony. I would like to make it easier for other women, so that is why I am writing this. I appreciate all those women who have already written books on menopause. However, I would stand in the health food store and look at all those books, and I would be confused as to which one to buy. It was all just overwhelming. My case was especially hard because I had to process my mother's death at the same time and I had no immediate family members left. Plus, I had been on birth control pills too long, and so my system did not know what it was doing when I went off them. In the end, the only way I got through it was by doing spiritual practices. Here are my suggestions:

Ask for Help

And I don't mean just from a doctor. Apparently there are many support groups available. I did not realize or think about that until the worst part was over. If you cannot find one, you might be able to create one. God will send you everyone you need, if you keep asking. You have never led a group? All you have to do is have every woman share and exchange ideas with each other and love each other. You *can* do this, at your home or wherever. Have the courage to ask friends and alternative healers to help you instead of suffering alone. Each woman could read up on the subject and give a book report. Each woman could study the rites of menopause in different cultures and try them.

For support, contact the North American Menopause Society at 440-442-7880 or visit their website at www.meno pause.org.

Be on a Strong Spiritual Path

If you are happy with your religion, go into it deeper. Maybe you can form a support group for menopausal women at your church. Singing would be good. Pray to expand your spiritual path to whatever is necessary. Most women tell me they are so grateful that they were students of metaphysics. For me, *A Course in Miracles* was the most helpful along with the rebirthing. Going to an ashram was important. Chanting in the temple is one of the best healing tools I know of. At one point I went to a spiritual group run by Jessica Dib in Baltimore and just let them take care of me. I am forever grateful because during that time I was too burned out to even work. Pat Waddell took care of me, and they all just loved me unconditionally. The whole group was on a spiritual path, and they considered it part of their karma yoga to look after me. It was amazing. I found a totally non-judgmental community.

Clear Up All Your Relationships

At any time, people in your family might be leaving the planet. I regretted so much that I was not able to complete my relationship with my sister before she died. She did not even make it through menopause. I had not even recovered from my sister's death when my mother died. Trying to handle all this in menopause was extremely difficult.

The spiritual masters say you are not really free until you release the family imprint. That is a very long process, and it takes a lot of spiritual work to do it. For me, menopause was all about releasing the intense family mind, and it took me a long time. One blessing I had was a friendship with a spiritual teacher in Spain, who told me it took her ten whole years to complete menopause. At the time she said it, I was shocked and did not think that would be the case for me, but it was.

Get Clear on the Issue of Death

If you are going for longevity, you have to study the philosophy of it, the psychology of it, and the physiology of it. If I had not had the knowledge of physical immortality under my belt, I think I would have given into aging, and then I would have been more depressed. Instead I used the time off to process my unconscious death urge—I went *through* it. I went through the dark night of the soul. It was a time of immense growth and learning.

When I came out on the other end, I was strong enough to write the book *Pele's Wish*, some of which is about the subject of physical immortality. During menopause, it is a wonderful time to study this whole subject.

Read Enlightened Books

Often I found the medical books on menopause too scary for me. Maybe that is because I was a nurse and it activated too much of the medical programming I had tried to erase. Here are some books I suggest:

- Texts from *A Course in Miracles*
- *Breaking the Death Habit,* by Leonard Orr

- *Beyond Mortal Boundaries,* by Anna Lee Skarin
- *The Lives and Teachings of the Masters of the Far East,* by Baird T. Spalding

Share Your Knowledge

Share with other women what works for you.

Engage in Rebirthing

See page 241.

Shave Your Head

This spiritual practice of *mundun,* having your head shaved, is one of the most powerful practices that I know. It is also a youthing process.

Follow Babaji's Formula for Happiness

It is truth, simplicity, love, and service to mankind—and the mantra. The mantra we chant is "Om Namaha Shivai," the highest thought in the universe, which means "I surrender to the God within [or Infinite Spirit, Infinite Being, and Infinite Manifestation]."

Value Seclusion and Silence

I made the mistake of not spending enough time alone at the beginning of menopause. This was a mistake, because after that I was forced to go into seclusion since I did not handle the first part right. An advanced teacher I met in Vienna finally ordered me to go into silence. Long periods of silence get you back into your true self.

The whole point I am trying to make is that menopause can be turned into a big "win."

My Personal Prayer

Praise to you, Divine Mother. You have once again made my life a miracle. I take refuge in your nurturing arms and compassion. I praise you for once again giving me a spirit of power and love and sound mind. I praise all you have created, and I want your name to be exalted.

You called me out of darkness to your marvelous light. I shout with the voice of triumph. I offer myself willingly to you. Great and marvelous are your works. May all nations worship before you! I fall down before you and worship you, who lives forever and ever; I praise you for your excellent greatness. With you, all things are possible. I am humbled and bowed down as you are revealed to me. You have destroyed the last enemy in me and have made me alive once again. You have raised me from the ash heap. I sing praises to your powers because you have revived my heart. You brought me back to life; therefore I glorify you in my spirit and body. Let me declare your glory among nations. I want to always obey your voice and be your treasure on this land. You have removed the burden from my shoulders.

As your servant, I will do your will from my heart. If

you will a thing for me to do, I will do it as perfectly as I can and give the glory to you. Let us all praise your name and greatness.

As a newborn baby, I desire the milk of our word. I have been born again, and I love you as an heir to your kingdom. Thank you for accepting my repentance and for giving me victory. You are my salvation. In you, Mother, I have peace. You have delivered me and put a new song in my mouth. I will serve you with gladness. I am lying at your divine feet and feeling pleased with the grace of your protection. You are the embodiment of ultimate bliss. You are supreme.

You have crowned my life with success and liberation. You are the essence of all that can be known. You are beyond comprehension. You have taken the form of my supreme Guru Babaji, by whose grace I have been allowed to live again. The love of your lotus feet gives me lasting happiness. Glory to you, O Mother of the Universe.

Everything I do is a result of your divine energy moving through me. I wish to express my appreciation to you as the source of all life. You are the breath of life; I am simply your instrument. You are my only goal in life. I desire that all should worship you day and night.

I offer up my song to nobody else but you.

I offer up my heart to nobody else but you.

My heart cries out for more of you.

My soul cries out for more of you.

My life is under your command.

I ask you to guide and assist me fulfilling the mission I volunteered to do on Earth prior to this embodiment. I open myself completely to you so that I can manifest what I vowed to accomplish during this incarnation. I agree to be part of cocreating the new world with you to the best of my ability. What shall we do, and how shall we do it? Show us the way.

Ignite us with illumination. I believe you will guide us. Oh, call on me. Show me what to write and say. Let the words of my mouth be acceptable to you. How can I convince humankind that *you are the answer*? I will tell the whole world of your irresistible miracles, and I pray that everyone will see that nothing is too hard for you.

It is you that can destroy the pain of this world. It is due to you that we will be able to release our sorrow. It is due to you that we shall find true happiness. On finding you, everything is found. You are the instrument of the healing of the world. May your knowledge triumph. Teach us all the language of your heart. Show us the way.

To you I give all the glory.

Love, Sondra Ray!

ABOUT THE AUTHOR

Sondra Ray is the bestselling author of many books, including *I Deserve Love* and *The Only Diet There Is*. One of the founders of the rebirthing movement, she is a workshop leader and devoted student of spiritual disciplines. She lives in Southern California. For more information, visit www .sondraray.com.

For information on the Loving Relationships Training and Rebirthing Worldwide, contact:

The New York and Philadelphia Rebirthing Centers
c/o Tony Lo Mastro and Maureen Malone
1027 69th Ave.
Philadelphia, PA 19126
215-424-4444 or 212-534-2969
tony.lomastro@verizon.net